DESIGNING YOUR LIFE

MARY B. COOK
A MEMOIR

DESIGNING YOUR LIFE

DYL Publishing books may be purchased for business, educational, personal, and
inspirational use. For in-depth information on all DYL Publications, please visit
us on Facebook.

Cover and interior art © M. Cook/J. Burr/J. Cibrone

FIRST EDITION   ISBN: 9780-0-9884-566-0-0

TABLE OF CONTENTS

INTRODUCTION

ACTS I

Introduction

I start by asking you to reflect on your life. You will realize it is shaped by the choices you make that range from the trivial to the heart wrenching. At the same time, our choices mold our worlds while they design our destinies. The tide of life can easily take you out or suck you in. Often, we overlook our choices and how they ultimately affect us.

I have witnessed many choices made in my life. Those not only made by myself - but by others. Some have been driven by false pretense based on emotions that play a part in our lives. Often times, subconsciously and unbeknownst to us, our life's choices are based and fed by temptation and other misguided thoughts. They drive and direct how we choose to react in life; therefore, we must recognize that setting aside one's *ego* in order to truly face our challenges can be our most difficult obstacle. Learning from selflessness through divine faith is not only a choice…. it's a way of life. The courage to choose life and/or death can be grueling for anyone who finds themselves in the grips of this type of conundrum.

Choosing absolute truth-in-self and demonstrating it in a respectful way is certainly a noble path. Finally, living to love and loving to live is perhaps one of the greatest choices we will ever make.

Please ask yourself: if we didn't have choices, how would we create our existence? It is clear that without unique choices we would all fit into the same mold; a mold of devastating similarity.

However, it is important for people to learn that we have the freedom to accept or reject individual choices made by our fellow man.

I have a saying, *"Embrace everyone's uniqueness as perfection."*

Additionally, one of our grandest choices is whether or not we believe in a great creator. I believe in a creator who gives humanity the gift of choice. So I ask you – if we don't believe in an ultimate creator, where might we find ourselves after death? It's my choice to believe that God has given humanity the gift of choice and the power to be creators. God expects us to do so.

By writing my life's story I hope to reach people in order to demonstrate how important every choice is: maybe the person I reach will be you.

I suggest we start by doing something that I call: *individual spiritual re-evolution.* Here and now, step back and evaluate your life. Begin to shape it through *well-thought-out* choices and by doing so – a beautiful new path will present itself.

Choose to love with great passion, sing and dance with great joy and choose to be honest even if it's the most difficult thing to do. *I hope you begin to make choices based on inherent wisdom and how you wish to be remembered.* You will come to realize that we all have the power to *design our lives*. Enjoy.

ACTS
PART I

A Life on Stage

As I drove into my garage the car was dripping with water from the rain that pelted us all the way home from the hospital. I can remember being the most exhausted I had ever been thus far since my journey began with this thing in my head. It was as though the bubble in my brain had totally sucked every emotion I ever had right out of my body. Wanting to get home to my wonderful cocoon, drop my suitcase and curling up in my soft warm bed was all I could focus on. I must be honest – I was giving up. The decision to let go of life was weighing down on me like a menacing concrete blanket. Giving up went against everything in my character; giving up was never an option. However — I had never been faced with a challenge like this.

Walking into the kitchen I sat my keys down on the counter and went to the refrigerator to get a bottle of water before lying down. I reached in for the water and turned to walk to my bedroom. Suddenly there it was: the beautiful picture of my mother and father. Immediate, transcendent warmth washed over me and absorbed my world with peace. That peace was exactly what I needed before heading off to bed. Before lying down, sitting on the edge of my bed and looking to the heavens, I said, "I am sorry, God, for making this decision. But I just can't go on like this anymore. I hope you will understand my choice and that you will help my family and me deal with whatever comes next."

As I slipped under my satin covers the exhaustion transformed into a magnificent feeling of gratefulness: I folded my hands and said a small prayer, I thanked God for my blessed life. At the end of my prayer I threw God a kiss and then slowly closed my eyes and drifted off into a soft peaceful slumber. Almost immediately I was swept into a vivid dream where I found myself in a grand amphitheater sitting beside a warm peaceful spirit. The spirit softly placed her hand on mine and she said, "Are you ready for us to share your life's experience with you?"

I said, "Well, I suppose so, but I really did want to rest first. My illness has been tiring so I just need a minute."

The spirit said, "Yes, we know you have been struggling. All you have to do is sit back and observe. That is all."

"I've never taken the time to step back and review my life. Maybe this will be good for me. Wait! What's the purpose of all this?"

The spirit said to me, "God has his reasons. We felt you needed to focus on something other than what you have been dealing with; that nasty thing in your head. Are you ready to begin?"

"You bet I am!" I politely said.

Then in my dream the clouds parted and there in front of me appeared a handsome young man of maybe 22 or 23 years. He was dressed in a neatly pressed dark suit as he stepped from a station wagon. The man had brownish auburn hair that was combed back from his reddish freckled complexion. He let out a hearty bellow, certainly a laugh that was unique from all other laughs. I recognized the laugh immediately as the man made his

way around the car. He opened the passenger side door
and out stepped a nun.

The angel asked, "Do you recognize the young
man?"

I said, "Absolutely, that's my Dad when he was
younger."

"Yes sweetie, it is. Did you know that he helped the
nuns at the hospital?"

"Yes, I did know that. He was always there because
of his job," I said.

She then asked me, "Do you know what he and your
grandfather did?"

"I sure do," I said with enthusiasm.

As my father and the nun entered the hospital, there
in the hall, walked a lovely young nurse. She had a Greta
Garbo look with crystal blue eyes that danced with
kindness and delight. Her skin played beautifully against
her soft curly brown hair. It was easy to notice the
seductive invitation that emanated from her warm smile; a

welcoming nature that easily accompanied the conviction of her fearless spirit. The young man and the nun made their way through the hall and passed by the nurse without a second glance.

I said to my angel, "Well that's a fine how do you do (I can't believe my dad walked right by her and didn't even notice). That's my mom when she was a young woman!"

"She is lovely."

I was captivated by the dream and I prayed that I wouldn't wake up. Seeing my parents at that age, so young and so full of life, touched my heart and stirred up powerful emotions. There before me in my dream was my future world being played out. I was witnessing a chance meeting between two incredible people that developed into a story that is O-F-T-B (*One for the Books*, as Dad always said).

The story begins…

The Nurse and the Musician

I couldn't have ordered more spectacular parents from the all-encompassing Spiegel catalog. Every day I make sure to thank God for their blessing. Not only did they adore each other but my mom and dad loved their entire family with unconditional love. Their love and faith brightly lit a path throughout their lives for those they loved to follow in. My parent's legacy started in the hospital where my mother worked as a nurse. My father would make routine trips to the hospital due to his family's long running profession: they were morticians. My father learned as my grandfather's understudy so one of his responsibilities was transporting the deceased from the hospital to the family mortuary. Unbeknownst to my dad, mom was studying to be a nurse and spending countless hours working at that very hospital. An ultimate design would bring them together.

Not only was dad working in the 'deceased' business but he was a musician as well. He and his friends formed a musical group and performed at a lounge across the street from the hospital. Dad was not only a saxophone and clarinet player but also had an incredible tenor singing voice. It was common for the nurses to frequent the lounge after a hard night's work for a little rest and relaxation. One evening, a certain young nurse decided to join the gang and head to the lounge; her brother decided to join in the fun and accompany her. The two loved dancing together and shared a special bond. The night was filled with great music and non-stop dancing. One-by-one, each nurse made her way up to the band to request a song. Not only did they want to dance to their song but also they especially wanted to hear it sung by the very talented and handsome lead singer. He was quite the crooner so the nurses swooned when he belted out their requests. It was the young nurse's first night at the lounge, so she made sure to request a popular piece of music that he might play. As time passed she didn't hear the song she requested – for some reason it was getting skipped over so she started to lose faith. The end of the night was quickly closing in. Then suddenly, she heard it. The crooner's amazing voice vibrated throughout the air and reached every corner of the lounge. The song, "A Small Hotel", was resonating in the young nurse's heart: she melted as he began to sing directly to her. After taking a moment to compose herself, she leaned over to her brother and said, "I'm going to marry that man."

The lounge became a great place for the nurse to mingle and relax with friends after that first magical night. After a while, the young nurse and crooner finally met and grew very fond of each other. Soon, the singer realized how special the nurse was so he asked her to the annual dance: *The May Frolic.* She accepted and began to wait in great anticipation for the big night to arrive. Please take into consideration the fact that the nurse worked at a Catholic hospital and her administrators were, of course, nuns. Therefore, the rules and regulations hovering over the nurses were a bit strict. Luckily, the crooner was a frequent face around the hospital and gained the love and respect of the hospital's administration. He would frequently run errands for them and often found himself chauffeuring the nuns about town. The holy administrators had a very special place in their hearts for this young, handsome musician/mortician!

Unfortunately, just a few weeks before the dance a number of nurses were caught breaking curfew. As punishment, they were confined to their duties in the hospital; meaning, they were forbidden to go to the dance! The young nurse longed to go with her handsome man so she was ultimately devastated. Her brother had bought her a beautiful dress so that she would look especially elegant for her date. It all seemed for not. Just when her spirit hit a low point, the mother Superior paid her a quick visit. Upon entering the nurse's room, the sympathetic nun noticed a beautiful dress hanging behind the door.

"Wow, Bernice! What a lovely dress. Is this yours?" asked the Mother Superior.

"Thank you. Yes, it's mine but it's for the dance and now I can't go," said Bernice.

"Well — who were you going to go with?"

"Henry La Croix had asked me to go," a downtrodden Bernice exclaimed.

Mother Superior asked, "Do you mean Henry La Croix, the young man that comes to help us all the time?"

"Yes"

"Well, let's see what we can do about this," she said in a soothing tone.

Bernice's anxiety was put to rest when she was permitted to attend the dance. When that long anticipated dance finally arrived, the two of them spent the entire night gliding across the floor in each other's arms. When the music stopped they didn't want the night to end, so Henry offered to walk Bernice home. I remember my dad telling me the story.

He said, "Your mother and I had such a great night so after the dance I didn't want to let her go; so I walked her back to the nurses' dorm. The streets were lit with soft moonlight that fell from the evening sky. I felt so at peace with her and I knew she was the one for me. I remember the radiating electricity I felt when I looked into her eyes. I was drawn in immediately, every time I gazed into those endless, deep blue ocean eyes. The feeling grew with each step and every time I looked away it was like I unplugged from a newfound energy-source. Can you imagine? I had never experienced chemistry like that with anyone. Those moments with Bernice were like listening to the perfect piece of music crafted by God himself, I couldn't breathe. I held her hand gently in mine as we made our way back to her house. I actually thought I was walking with an angel. As we stood under the soft moonlight, I wrapped my arms around her waist, brought her close and gave her the kiss of a lifetime. I knew then and there that I would spend the rest of my life with her."

That magical, moonlit evening sparked a legacy. Henry and Bernice's marriage and undying love has always and will continue to deeply affect the multitudes of people they've touched. Mom and Dad, we all thank you.

Henry and Bernice LaCroix

The Closet

My Cheshire eyes peered above my crib's edge to survey my surroundings. I remember my petite room and my earliest years as if it was yesterday. My room overwhelmed me with comfort and engrained the idea that the world was consumed with absolute pure love. The room housed my crib, my little home. It came to be that spending time there, as I believed it, was like being on stage: I felt like a performer that was given a small space to entertain. I expected each one of my family members and friends to come and visit me. At times, I can still remember standing up tall and peeking over the side of the crib, just waiting for my next visitor to arrive. I relished and basked in their attention and just couldn't get enough. Now, as an adult, I realize how fortunate I was to have had such a nice environment to grow up in. It was a place that didn't teach me negativity but only taught me how to love and care unconditionally.

Outside of my room came the constant sound of music; those great sounds became a fixture at our family and neighborhood gatherings. I remember those beautiful sounds blanketing me with waves of soft silk. Inevitably, my parent's love for music filtered down through the ranks of their children and grandchildren.

The LaCroix house was always jumping: Party, party and more partying. One person became two; two people became four and four people turned into a blend of laughter and the feeling of old friends being made. The glowing sound of fun would inevitably waft through the air and find its way to my ears. I stood in my crib wondering and dreaming about what was happening in the great beyond. What could all of this commotion be? One consistent feeling I remember liking was the excitement and fun of it all. Needless to say our neighbors and friends knew they could always come to the LaCroix home for a party.

"Wow!" That's what I thought as I listened to the laughter outside my door. I asked myself, "How could they neglect me by keeping the door closed?" It was like an iron wall that separated me from an indescribable world of fun. How could I convince whoever was outside the door to recognize I was there and wanted to be in the center of things? I cried, whimpered and screamed. I did everything I could think of to get someone's attention. Then finally! One of my parent's friends would eventually come to ogle over me or my mom would come remind me that I was supposed to be sleeping. I could only hope that they wouldn't leave before picking me up and whisking me away to join the party. "Well, alright, but just for a minute," my mom would say with a warm smile. Finally, I figured out how to convince those adults to believe that children needed to be seen and not just heard! Upon my escape, I was whisked away to a world where I met musicians, great singers and countless other extremely colorful characters that buzzed around the house.

My head swam with the sounds of laughter that swirled around me. Mom snuggled me into her lap to watch our jovial guests perform and also play cards (a favorite LaCroix past-time). Climbing down from her lap I would crawl into the kitchen to listen to my dad and his friends sing — that is what I truly loved. What an incredible world I was a part of. After getting used to that level of fun, I could have hung with the best of them. Unfortunately, the fun always had its limits so sooner rather than later, my mom would scoop me up and carry me back to bed.

My mom would always say with a beautiful smile, "Well, you managed to get in the thick of things again! Now go to sleep little girl." She put me to bed with incredible hugs and kisses that allowed me to dream of the next marvelous party. My parent's fun spirits stretched far and wide; they were the toast of the town and loved entertaining people. The best times around the LaCroix home were definitely Sundays after church when we would gather for great food and some rock-n-roll. My family immersed itself in music with my father leading the troops; he was an amazing musician who loved playing the saxophone, clarinet and sang with a strong tenor voice that could knock your socks off. He and a few of his closest friends decided to form a barbershop quartet. It was a tight knit unit that when once got going was impossible to slow down: Nor did anyone want to! A few drinks didn't hurt the good times at all. When coming over to the LaCroix house everyone knew dad would be playing his heart out and mom would be dancing up a storm. Yes, my mother was the dancer of the family; a non-stop whirlwind of fun.

I used to fear that she would whip up little tornados all over the house, especially when dancing with Henry. Come to think of it, I don't recall Henry dancing much. He would just stand still as mom danced circles around him. Above all else, dad and his musical pals knew how high to turn the dial before things began to get out of control. At all costs, a raucous and fun time was my parent's main goal.

Those nights were always filled with music and laughter until the day gave way to night. In the morning, I was always surrounded by the hustled and bustle of my six siblings racing around my room: a flurry of activity swarmed around me, I could never quite figure out why. I didn't realize that my bedroom sort of doubled as a walk-in closet for my six siblings. Yes, six siblings! Add my mom and dad to the mix and there were nine people scrambling around me getting ready for the day. The size of my family led my parents to creatively use that larger than life walk-in closet as my bedroom. Henry and Bernice consistently made the best out of any situation – the room was perfect for me. You might think I would have been upset or bothered due to the lack of privacy in my room, but it was just the opposite. My unique living arrangement was a blessing in disguise, it created a world of opportunities for me to interact with and perform for my family. Seeing my brothers and sisters coming and going was such an exhilarating feeling. When they came in, I knew I was going to receive a huge "Hello Mary!" I loved hearing my sisters talk about the news of the day and also listening to my parent's soft voices as they laid me to sleep.

Little Me

I look back on those times and realize that I wasn't raised by the T.V. set or other common childhood distractions. My youth was shaped by the caring nature of my siblings and parents; those precious interactions shaped my world. With their wisdom and encouragement, my family helped me establish an unshakeable foundation that supported me in taking my next steps into my life's journey.

Walk On the Wild Side

Strength and courage were instilled in me when I was very young. You will find that strength is a theme that continues on throughout this book. My family was and always will be my support system. One first glimmer of their support was when I took my first steps as a little toddler roaming around my parent's house. You read those words correctly: I can actually remember some of my first steps. It might be hard to believe but it's quite vivid as I look back. I was in the family dining room grasping and wobbling along just as any other "beginner" would be accustomed to doing. Sputtering and spattering, I would pull myself up onto a yellow leather chair and would hold on for dear life.

Over the years, I've categorized one method of thinking as: "Failing Forward'. To 'Fail Forward', we must learn and gain wisdom through the mistakes we make and the challenges we encounter. I've always felt that if I don't at least try something then I have already failed.

When I saw that toy I knew that a challenge lay ahead. As I remember it, the toy was at the foot of another chair in the distance. To get it, I had to make my way through the dining room and into the living room: how could I do it? According to my toddler calculations, the small distance seemed to be several continents away. I distinctly remember an immense desire to have that toy, knowing it would bring me such joy and happiness. I was set to go and the idea of failing wasn't an option. Above all else, I believed no harm could come from trying. My toddler mind was beginning to form a plan: the plan was to try and mimic what the adults were doing and to use my legs to prop myself up in a standing position. I would then move my legs just as they did –

That was it! I began my quest: one foot out then another foot down, mission accomplished. Second foot in front of the first, second foot down. I felt that I was doing such a great job. Only one more giant step for girl-kind and the toy was mine. As my little white baby shoes scuttled across the floor I could sense something special was happening. And finally, I did it. I grabbed that toy and basked in its glory. From the color of the soft beige carpet beneath my feet to the feeling of accomplishment, I still relive that moment from time to time.

It was that feeling of success that I liked; the sense of doing something new and gratifying. I wanted to repeat and incorporate that feeling in everything I did. So there I was, able to take little baby steps to explore new frontiers.

Although I had a happy childhood, it didn't go without its share of pain and mishaps. I like to compare my youth to a fairy tale. Fairy tales are often thought of as being pleasant and ending with the most positive of outcomes. However, after a second glance, you will see that many fairy tales don't go without insurmountable challenges. We need to first recognize, adapt to and then attack these great hurdles in order to overcome them. Throughout this book I will talk about the challenges I've faced and how I chose to handle them. I've received and I do admit that I was given a foundation that fostered and nurtured many positive opportunities, for that I'm grateful. I guess you could say I'm the extremely **Lucky #7**....

Lucky # 7

From the time I could form a coherent thought, I was aware of the loving family that surrounded me. As I matured I recognized a sense of bonding with my siblings and parents. We were growing into a powerful entity. The years went by and we all became closer and closer, almost acting as a well-oiled machine. When one of our family members was absent the rest of the group was greatly affected: the family was an engine that needed every one of its pistons to fire in order to run smoothly. Being the youngest of seven children caused the need for me to have everyone together in order to feel secure; there truly was an unspoken connection within our family.

The eldest of the LaCroix clan is my caring and vivacious sister, Carol. There is a curious thing about our relationship; it's the fact that there are 16½ years between us. When we are introduced to people for the first time, I always make sure to let everyone know that she is the eldest. That line always pushes her button and results in me getting that classic, agitated look of hers. Being the oldest, Carol naturally gravitated towards taking care of her brothers and sisters as though they were her own children. I was only 1½ when she decided to go away to college, but her move didn't last long enough for me to start worrying about her. After a short spell, Carol soon realized the collegiate life wasn't one she wished to pursue, so she chose to return home in order to find local employment. Soon thereafter, Carol and her boyfriend decided to tie the knot. When Carol started having children (which came to a total of six), I was all but 4½ years old. To this day all of her children seem like my brothers and sisters, rather than my nieces and nephews.

The second oldest LaCroix child is my brother, Norm. When I was only three he broke my heart and headed off to college. It seemed like an eternity would pass between his trips home. I can remember waiting in between the front door and the window curtain, just waiting in excited anticipation for his return (sometimes he would bring a friend home to add to the fun). Norm and I always had an incredible connection. He was the steady, self-assured type that never seemed to waiver. Most importantly, he was very good at alluding trouble; he never got caught with his hand in the proverbial cookie jar.

His elusive behavior would aggravate my other brother Denny enormously. Denny, on the other hand, was almost too good at getting into trouble and sometimes found himself in hot water. I feel confident in saying that Denny is the zaniest of the LaCroix brood. He's always joking and is the epitome of the "happy-go-lucky" personality. No matter the situation Denny could always brighten a room, all while containing his endearing gruff ways. He gave me so much loving attention that I really did begin to think that life was "all about me" (so it's his fault). Still a kid at heart, Denny is always a riot to be around.

When Denny was away from family gatherings, I always felt his absence. One particular time I felt that overbearing absence was when he and his friend Butch (who is now my brother-in-law), decided to join the U.S. Navy. It was an earth shaking experience, not only for me, but for my whole family. That occasion marked the first time one of our "pistons" would be extracted from the engine entirely (joining the military proved much different than heading off to college). I was devastated and albeit selfish, all I could ask was, "How could he leave? What's going to happen now?" I didn't understand, nor did I want to accept the fact that those are the things that happen naturally in life. Family members leave the nest as life moves along. It was just a matter of time before our troops started to move on, and move on they did. When Denny left the household I remember that I longed for the love and camaraderie I once shared with him. I didn't understand that he was doing something for his future and for the welfare of our country. I forced myself to be patient in waiting for his return and that's exactly what I did. I believed that if I just sat there long enough, it would be plenty to force my brother to appear in our front walkway.

It was like heaven when Denny returned home on leave. He would come up to my room, lean over my bed and give me a huge hug and I felt like he would never let go. Those great hugs always produced so many tears. After taking some time to talk with me, Denny would dig into his satchel and bring out the greatest gifts. I must admit that I always looked forward to Denny's visits, in part, to find what amazing things he brought back from all corners of the world (getting those gifts would somehow stop me from crying). No matter where I am or no matter what I'm up against, I know that big brother will always be there to help me.

My beautiful sister Bernadette is the middle child, but in no way does she suffer from the fabled 'middle-child' syndrome. I feel Bernadette is most like our mother because of the fact that she is an extremely loving and giving person. She has such a strong and independent sense of self that sometimes Bernadette makes up her own words that almost turn into their own language. When she starts to rattle off those new and interesting words, we can't help but laugh at the puzzling looks she puts on people's faces. Somehow I completely understand what she is saying (which actually scares me sometimes). Bernadette has such a great way about her, part of her glowing essence is in the way she is able to poke fun at herself. She is my angel in so many ways. My sister's love will be on display throughout this book.

Now I have the daunting task of describing my brothers Fred and Gary. I will immediately say that Fred is one of the most positive and progressive individuals one could ever meet. He finds positive reinforcement through many vehicles: his family, his talents and certainly through his faith in our creator. I feel it's his glowing outlook on life that benefits not only his mental health, it lends to his physical stability as well. Believe it or not, Fred has somehow avoided the many typical illnesses in life. Also, like many of my family members, Fred is a world-class musician who specializes in percussion and sings like Michael Buble. Without a doubt, he was blessed with my father's DNA. My dad used to say that he loved playing music with Fred because it always made dad into a better musician.

My brother Gary is the second to the last of the LaCroix family. Gary is a lovely human being filled with talent that is hard to describe. His voice is like heaven and he can play the keyboards like nobody's business. He was born with an uncanny ability to pick up any instrument and begin playing it as if he had played it forever. What an entertainer. He is also the spiritual leader of our family, his warmth and inner-kindness is felt instantly when you meet him.

Now a little bit about me: when I introduce myself to people I usually find myself saying, "I'm the youngest of seven". It's become a position and identity that I've become proud of. Most people think that because I'm the baby of the family I must be have been spoiled. On the flip side, I think being the youngest of seven granted me the opportunity to connect with my family in a different way than most people ever get to experience.

If my parents weren't near to me then one of my siblings was always there to shower me with the attention I needed. I remember the early days of sitting on the sofa and constantly having someone there to play with me (again, it was a stage for me to perform on). Those times allowed me to establish a friendship with my brothers and sisters, letting me see them as individuals, not just family. I like to think my personality developed from those experiences and ultimately from the mixture of my siblings combined influences. Each of them is vastly different from the other so I wanted to emulate everything they did. It wasn't easy but I tried and I like to think that I've succeeded in some ways.

My brothers and sisters are gifts from God. By observing their unique traits, I've learned how to become somewhat of a chameleon throughout my life. The key to survival is adapting to one's environment and evolving as a person. If one works on their personal growth, they will hopefully develop into a fulfilled and happy person: A happiness that radiates from one's spirit. I feel my family has taught me that crucial life lesson.

So there you have it, a quick low-down on the...

La Croix bunch: all except for one furry little addition...

It's a Doggie Dog World

The LaCroix kids certainly formed the core heartbeat of our family. But as is common with any jovial and passionate family, we always made room for more. We adopted a puppy one holiday season, a beagle that quickly became one of the best family pets in so many ways. Our furry little friend was a Christmas present one snowy year. I remember jumping on the bed with Gary when we both heard a barking in the distance. We were so excited that we began to scour the house in hopes to find the culprit. We searched and we searched, unfortunately, our efforts turned up nothing.

That year on Christmas morning, all of the LaCroix kids raced down to the tree to discover what might be awaiting us. I was puzzled when I found a box under the Christmas tree that sounded like it was whimpering; upon further inspection, I saw that the box had a moist nose popping through the top. In a flash, out sprung a tiny puppy with a big red bow around its neck. The pup was instantly welcomed as a new addition to the family, we named our new gift, Cindy. She was simply adorable and the type of dog who could talk to you with her eyes. With just a passing glance she would let us know if she was hungry, tired or ready for a run in the yard. Our cute little pooch taught me to understand the world more deeply through simple movements and gestures.

One of Cindy's most coveted pieces of furniture was a brown chair that was nestled in our living room. Our puppy was fearless when it came time to claim what was rightfully hers so when an intruder would sit in her chair, Cindy quickly let them know it wouldn't be tolerated. The ferocious beagle (well, not so much) would swagger over in front of them, sit down, slowly tilt her head and look directly into the person's eyes. Without a bark or a grunt she would say with a longing look, "What the heck do you think you're doing in my chair?" Don't fool yourself, my family members and I would get the same treatment. We all knew better to try and sit in Cindy's chair when she was around. Our boisterous beagle was certainly the master of her domain.

Cindy became the eighth member of our family... pets often do. Our furry little friends become like children or best friends to their owners. Cindy was an incredible little puppy who gained my love through teaching me to communicate on so many levels.

It wasn't long before Cindy's larger-than-life personality began to garner attention all over town. Our town was so safe that she could take walks alone whenever she pleased. One of her favorite destinations was our town's post office that was located in the heart of downtown. The postmaster knew Cindy well and would always greet her with a treat and some water. After a brief visit and some well-deserved petting, she would be on her way again. Cindy became so loved that if she would wander too far, neighbors would quickly let us know of her whereabouts. It seems unfathomable that such a safe environment could exist in today's society. In fact, our pup was so comfortable that she chose to make the postman's door her final resting place. One day we received a phone call telling us Cindy made a trip downtown to say one last good-bye to the postman. It was then and there that she decided to take her final rest. I miss you Cindy...

Charlie Puckett

Growing up in a small community of only 1,500 people was a unique and dynamic experience. In our cozy little town, cradled away in a quite area of northern Michigan, it was common to say hello to a fellow neighbor as though everyone were life-long friends. It was a community where people genuinely cared for each other and would go the extra step in lending a helping hand. I realize how important small towns are in the make-up of modern American culture. I can certainly attest to the fact that many relationships that grew from my little city were one of a kind.

One of my closest friends, Kathy, grew up right across the street. She and I were introduced when we were just babies and over the years our friendship has grown into a sisterhood. Kathy has become just like one of the family. The bond we share has taught us one thing; that we always have someone in life to lean on. That and other relationships that I formed during my childhood were often forged every morning when I made my way to school. Although we had to cross a very dangerous highway on our walk, we always felt safe and sound because of the presence and watchful eyes of one man: Charlie Puckett.

Charlie was our wonderful and very brave crossing guard. He was larger than life. As a little girl I remember looking up at him as he wore a policeman's uniform and had three very large *chins*. From his plumb-round face protruded a magnificent, shining white smile. He somehow smiled all the while speaking to people in a raspy voice. The only thing larger than Charlie was his wonderful kind spirit. I felt safe and secure when he wrapped his huge hand around my little paw before we set out across the treacherous highway. I tried to keep in step with the way Charlie would sway as he walked us across the road. Charlie was not just a crossing guard but a safe-keeper and man who truly loved what he did every day. As he walked us across the road it was evident that he did so with great joy in his heart. Rain, sleet, or snow, our hero never missed a day.

I learned many things on those early morning walks with Charlie. One important thing he taught me was that it is absolutely possible for a person to enjoy what they do for a living. Our big protector found that by displaying kindness and goodwill towards others, it brought him satisfaction and joy. Charlie's kindness and protection made a big impact on my friends and me. Through Charlie's actions, I now realize how much of an impact adults have on children; even in the smallest cases. What may seem to be a trivial moment to adults; may actually have an everlasting effect on children. I've learned that we're responsible to have positive impacts on all of our children.

Although Charlie did his best to protect us from danger on that treacherous highway, unfortunately, I will always remember an accident that occurred (with difficulty, I will explain). On an unassuming crystal-blue morning, just a few blocks from where Charlie was working, an adorable young boy was killed in an auto accident. The news hit me hard and it affected the entire community. Sadly, I learned that the cute boy was someone I babysat for many times. For some unknown reason, the young boy tried to cross the road without Charlie's assistance about two blocks from where Charlie's post was. The boy darted into the road and because of that simple mistake we lost a precious little soul. Being a young girl who was sheltered from such tragedies, it was especially painful to say goodbye to my little friend. His family was similar to mine in that it was very large. I couldn't possibly imagine the pain they were feeling. I know that Charlie, in all of his years, never came to terms with what occurred that tragic day.

Now, when I see crossing guards protecting our children from harm, I always extend the greatest amount of respect to them. They hold our children's lives in their hands. We all love you Charlie!

An Apple A Day

After crossing the highway on my way to school, I would pass a grocery store. The owners of the store would place huge baskets of fruit and vegetables along their front walk. I can remember a particularly long and busy school day when I didn't find time to eat. Come day's end, I was famished and left the school grounds starving. As I raced home for something to munch on, a burning began to grow in my belly with each passing footstep. Then – there it was, right in front of me: outside of the little grocery store lay a huge basket of apples. My hungry eyes zeroed in on one delicious piece and I quickly scooped it up and continued walking as if nothing happened.

With my new criminal life underway I continued walking towards Charlie Puckett. He took my empty hand while I grasped the apple in the other as we set out across the road. During that routine walk, however, there was something brewing beneath the surface. Something was getting to me. The feeling of an over-powering guilt swallowed my conscience.

"This apple isn't mine!" I thought.

I had stolen it and now I was on the other side of the law. My innocent mind couldn't shake the awful feeling as Charlie saw me off towards my house. The guilt began to sink deeper and deeper into my already aching stomach. It was all too much for me to handle so I decided to right the wrong I had done; I decided to return the apple to its proper place. As I approached Charlie, he looked down and said, "Little Ms. Mary... Did you forget something?" With my head bowed I said, "Yes Charlie. I forgot to be honest. I took this apple and it isn't mine. I shouldn't have taken it."

Charlie was part of the police force and had the power to send me up the river. He took my little hand as I trembled and said, "O.K. Let's get this back to where it belongs before it is too late."

I made my way back to the grocery store, back to the scene of the crime; and for a moment I thought the police would be there with guns drawn while helicopters circled above.

I thought, "I don't ever want to feel this again!"

In many ways I'm no different than most people. I'm no saint. I admit that when I was young sometimes I tried my hand at the occasional white lie. However, I learned quickly that guilt always followed my indiscretions, whether they were big or small. That one tiny apple taught me an important lesson; that sometimes we're unable to obtain things that simply aren't meant to be ours. That lesson also instilled the importance of honesty within me. I learned that we must be honest, even if it's the hardest thing you do. I devote myself every day in being honest and truthful. Now and then I may stumble, but it's a choice of how I want to represent myself and how I choose to be remembered. This is valuable key in life that would be joyfully played out.

The Piano

The power and beauty of music was a constant great presence in the LaCroix household. Melodic and sinuous notes floated through the house; those tones made me want to learn to play an instrument so I could join in the fun. I chose to take up the piano and started formal lessons in the first grade. Now I can't say that I was a natural on the piano but I felt I was progressing quite nicely. After three years of lessons I was getting the hang of things and started to feel confident in my piano prowess. Well, that feeling came crashing down when my older brother Gary decided to take up the piano as well. He took to the keys quickly and was knocking out great music in no time. To sum up Gary's musical talents in a few short words, it would go something like this: he is a freak of nature! Gary's effortless talent came to light during his first week of beginner lessons. The day came for one of his first lessons with a tutor, but he didn't have the first year lesson book that was required. Me, being the generous sister that I am (☺), I let him take my third yearbook just so he would have something to work with. What a mistake that was! His manic and magical fingers made their way through the advanced lessons so quickly that it made people's heads spin. Gary progressed at such a rapid pace that I couldn't keep up. I hate to admit that it was Gary's mastery of the piano that led me to stop taking lessons and focus on other musical ventures (somewhere, there is a small violin playing). I admit to a bit of sibling rivalry, so to my chagrin, Gary was Mozart's second coming.

With that God given talent Gary developed not only into a talented piano player but also into a gifted entertainer. His knack to pick up any instrument and play as though he were a seasoned pro is uncanny. So can you tell me: how is that? It may sound like I was green with envy, but as you read further you will understand my pain. Throughout our childhood, Gary and I not only learned music together but performed side-by-side as well. Our outfit consisted of him jamming away on the keyboards, Fred rocking the drums, and me signing my heart out. As a trio, I felt that we had an explosive musical chemistry. Although blessed with that great musical talent, somehow, Gary was a victim of the dreaded 'stage-fright'. Performance after performance, he always tried to hide from the limelight by shying away and using the keyboards as a shelter.

Gary was somewhat reserved in the public eye but it didn't mean he never acted on his ambitions. There was a time when he and his drummer friend, Lenny, agreed to move to Rochester, N.Y. and perform on a regular basis. Our entire family had faith in the dynamic duo, but before they left Michigan I made sure to impart some wisdom upon my brother. I recommended he give singing a chance so that their shows consisted of more than just their incredible instrumentals. Gary took my advice and set off for New York in hopes of discovering a new talent. It only took that short time for him to uncover a fantastic singing voice that he was always too shy to express. When they returned, Gary belted out a few songs that blew my hair back. He did it again. That voice was unbelievable, almost angelic. With that new weapon in his musical arsenal, all I could do was throw my hands in the air, sit back and enjoy my brother's amazing talents and love every minute of it! Now the fairy tale becomes even more colorful.

Fairy Tales Come True

I had fun as a kid but just like anyone else, I was faced with challenges and struggles. Perhaps the most difficult hurdle to clear was learning my father was diagnosed with colon cancer when I was only eight years old. That horrific news sent a collective, disparaging sigh throughout my family. The idea of my dad falling to a deadly disease didn't sink in until doctors informed us they were giving him only a short time to live. The news struck my heart deeply. At that moment I was aware of how severe the situation had become.

Dad's body became extremely fragile as the cancer broke him down – we helplessly watched as he lost a frightening amount of weight. It's an arduous task explaining how it felt to watch my 'Superman' begin to fade before me. I knew he was sick, but at such a young age I remember thinking that getting sick was simply coming down with a cough or a stomachache. Thankfully, my mother was always there to weather the storm when things got tough. By showing her unconditional positivity and strength through her unwavering spirituality, our family stayed strong. Our 'Superwoman' held firm in her belief that God was and always would be with us.

When dad was first diagnosed with cancer, mom took it upon herself to gather the troops so that she could ready everyone for the battle of a lifetime. It was our mother's love and perseverance that carried our family through those rigid times. At one point during my father's hospitalization she held a three-day-vigil by his bedside. Countless hours were spent praying in hopes that God would grant my dad the strength needed to overcome the illness. As visitors came and went, she held strong by his side and continued to search for a miracle. After numerous medical setbacks and many heartfelt prayers, God began to shine his light on my mother's faith. Slowly but surely signs of my dad's health improving began to show. Then finally, after what seemed to be a long and rigorous journey, my family received a phone call from the doctors telling us that the cancer had gone into remission. It was a call sent by God.

We rejoiced and let out screams that surely reached up to the heavens. Mom dedicated her entire life and her whole being to our family. It was a powerful act to observe. Her deep faith was mirrored not only by our family, but was felt by people who were in the presence of her radiating love. I learned many things at that young age; one was that we truly have the power to change our destiny through faith. I'm fortunate to have witnessed its power and feel that my faith in God has undeniably helped me in constructing my life's design.

The Beach Front

Lake Huron holds a special place in my heart. My parents would take our family there to visit our grandparents almost once a month. Those mini-vacations filled my days with incredible memories; most of those memories were certainly meaningful while others are simply hysterical. My grandfather loved going by 'Grandpa Kakai' and my grandmother went by 'Grandma Zozo'. Their home was large enough to keep our entire family comfortable because they also had five cabins nearby for the family to use for vacationing. I remember countless days waking up to a pristine crystal lake with the early morning sun dancing on its subtle waves. My grandparents invited every member of our family, each and every one – they made sure to post an open lake policy. Our boisterous brood would fill the days by fishing, swimming and throwing incredible parties. Oh, those were the days.

Fishing was huge in our family and was like a religion. A few of my family members liked to consider their talents good enough to be labeled as 'master fishermen'. They enjoyed every aspect of the sport and did everything from regular fishing and smelt dipping to cleaning and preparing the catch – they did it all. We had a blast standing side-by-side cleaning hundreds of perch after a smooth day on the water. Smelt dipping was a family favorite (to my chagrin). I remember a specific time when my dad's brother, Uncle Tom, took me out to teach me the mysteries of smelt dipping. If you are unfamiliar with smelt dipping, here's a crash course.

First, smelt are small silvery fish that are approximately six inches long. The dipping (fishing) is done sometime in early April late at night in the secluded rivers that flow from the great lakes. In order to start dipping properly, the fisherman needs to sling a bucket over his shoulder while having a net ready in-hand (and if he wants to stay dry, a nice over-sized pair of waders is critical!). The basic idea of smelt dipping is to dip your net into the water, scoop up a huge number of the silvery suckers and then with one continuous motion, raise them from the river and into a bucket. Sounds rather simple doesn't it?

Well, when it comes to smelting the idea is the bigger the net, the bigger the bounty will be; however, with a big net must come a big fisherman. Unfortunately, at the age of 11, my net was nearly twice as big as me and weighed more than a hippo (well it seemed to me). That evening the fish were running well and although I was wrestling with the net, I started to wrangle some of the little buggers. Since I wasn't very strong at the time I couldn't swing the fish directly in the bucket with one fluid motion. That forced me to transfer the smelt to the bucket using only my hand. BIG MISTAKE!

My uncle warned me," No! Don't put your hand in the net! Just tip it and let the smelt slide into the bucket. No hands in the net!"

As it turned out I should have listened to that spectacular advice because the next time I dipped my hand in I was greeted by a very large and nasty eel. It wrapped itself around my arm tightly with its slimy body as I screamed my fool head off. Uncle Tom thought a great white shark was lurking in the water because of my panicked screams (sorry Uncle Tom). To me, the eel was just as nasty and frightening as any shark could have been. Fortunately, he came to my rescue and released me from the beast's grip. I haven't been smelt dipping since!

Those times on Lake Huron were priceless because I learned how magical and precious the environment can be: it has the power to bring families together. When those days at the lake were done, I made my way inside and usually went straight to climbing up on my grandpa Kakai's chair. It was the best seat in the house to listen to his magnificent stories. Grandpa Kakai was a bellowing boisterous man who smoked his pipe while telling stories filled with magic and wonder. He always spoke with great energy and breathed life into each one of his stories. One of the most interesting focused on the family business – the business of being morticians. It's not as cryptic as is sounds. My family has been involved in the mortuary business for several generations. I find that most people are taken aback when they hear about some of our family stories.

One night, grandpa Kakai explained that as a young boy one of his responsibilities was to help his father prepare the recently departed for their funeral. My great grandparents' home was located at one part of the property while the mortuary was several acres away on another – so if his father needed his help they had to use the mortuary's bell to signal home. Through his stories I learned that grandpa Kakai often heard the bell ringing in the middle of the night (can you imagine, being woken up by death?). My grandfather was forced to climb over fences and race across the field with only the stars above him watching. Those runs were such adventures that he even had to hurtle livestock and use the moon's guiding light for direction. One night, under that same dim moonlight, he told the story of something very creepy and unfortunate that happened out in the fields.

Grandpa Kakai said, "I was running like the wind. I climbed over one fence and then another. Then with a blind leap of faith I took one last hurdle and oh what a hurdle it was! I landed smack dab in the middle of dead cow! I was literally up to my knees in hamburger!"

I yelled, "Holy cow!"

My eyes blew up into saucers as he gyrated and bounced up and down in his chair while describing the cow's innards. My imagination ran wild when grandpa became excited and went on his little rampages while telling tales. They are vivid stories that still resonate throughout my family. Grandpa Kakai and grandma Zozo were incredible people whose vivacious lifestyles will be shared from generation to generation. My time with my grandparents taught me many life lessons. One of which is that death is an extension of life (I will touch more on that later).

Grandpa Kaki and Grandma Zozo

Let's Go to the Lake

Life by the lake was so much fun that my parents finally decided to buy a lakefront cottage of their own. The humble abode was only 12 miles from our house so it was easy to spend weekends and summers enjoying its beauty. I felt like we were going to heaven every time my dad let us know we were packing up the car and going to the lake. My favorite lake adventure was water skiing, a tricky little skill that my brother Fred taught me at the ripe age of five. I was so small he could drag me around the lake behind my dad's tiny fishing boat (my little frame only needed a seven horse power engine). Anyone who caught a glimpse of us out on the water thought it was hysterical; all they saw was an itty-bitty girl being slung around the lake. For heaven's sakes, the skies were even bigger than I was.

Not only did the lake provide one of the best landscapes for outdoor fun, but the remote location provided my family with a quiet place to grow as musicians. We transformed the garage into something that resembled a 'mini-Woodstock'. My brothers made that small area their own universe to perform and perfect their craft. Over the summers we would throw wild blow outs that became quite popular. Catching wind of the tunes, our neighbors came running every time my family fired up the sound. Those nights attracted all types of people from the area – from friends who just wanted to party to other local musicians who wanted to join the jam sessions. Some of those bashes saw nearly 50 crazy kids running around in their adolescent glory. Those parties resonated across the lake as night flipped to the morning light.

Those rhapsodic Saturdays gave way to my mom's favorite day: Sunday Funday. Sunday was the day she showed off her 'fish-frying' talents. Dad would wake up early in the morning, hit the lake and return to the cottage with a bounty of fish that would make us all come running.

"I caught a boat load this morning! Get the kids together!" dad would yell.

It's easy to say that we were spoiled by my parent's infamous 'fish-fries'. This was truly the way my mom showed her love for family and friends. Everyone would return to our house to rant about the fun they had the night before as we all gorged ourselves on mounds of walleye.

Those feasts were always followed by another jam session that lasted into the night. To me, it seemed like the party never stopped.

Our family getaways were incredible, it was a time that let me explore the world and grow into my own skin. I made such great friends who sometimes taught me about a big glorious world that lay outside of my comfort zone. In particular, I can still remember two very unique friends I made one summer. I was about 13 years old when I made their acquaintance. They were from the big city of Detroit and were the first friends I had made who were actually from a major metropolis. They were sisters: Susan and Denise. Their beauty was the first thing I noticed and the second was how differently they were dressed. As I introduced myself I was mesmerized by how their long silk-like hair flowed over their beautiful blouses. I was immediately intrigued by the city slickers and could instantly sense that we came from different backgrounds. They were city girls while I hailed from a more rustic scene.

Although we came from opposite worlds – Susan, Denise and I became great friends over the years. Every summer we would meet and share our stories about what had happened over the winter. It wasn't until we all felt comfortable that my kind friends and I shared our first impressions of each other. I let them know how enamored by their beauty I was at first site (in part because as a young girl I always felt challenged in the 'looks' department). I also loved to borrow their clothes from time to time; especially the girl's many cool bathing suits. You could say that I had a 'flare' for fashion, as I was quite the gregarious dresser. I loved wearing wide brimmed floral hats with bright sun colored blouses that were topped off with a pair of over-sized rimmed sunglasses. My curly locks would fall freely upon my shoulders and that was one aspect of my appearance that stood out from other girls. At that time, having long straight hair parted down the middle was all the rage. However, my curls would sometimes kink up and force me to spend time trying to straighten things out. Susan and Denise were truthful when they told me my vibrant fashion statements sort of 'freaked them out'. With them being from the city, I proved to be a newfound entity that they were trying to get used to. Although different in appearances, we bonded quickly.

Susan and Denise said to me, "You were so friendly to us! It was so nice of you because we were new and didn't know anyone. Thank you for being so inviting."

They appreciated the fact that I went out of my way to introduce them to many of my friends. I found it easy to open up and trust them enough to welcome them into my circle.

Over the next few years Susan and my brother Fred became close. Within three years of getting to know each other, the two decided to tie the knot. Today, I'm lucky to be able to call Susan my sister-in-law. Through those contemporary city slickers, I learned that being open and honest in new relationships is the best recipe for happiness.

Many of those friendships at the lake taught me how to trust and be trusted by my peers. My new friends and I were so different that it was not only necessary but critical to break down personal barriers in order to have some fun.

Once those barriers were torn down, fun was all we had to worry about. Playing in those warm summer breezes taught me how to accept each and every friend as my own. That example of forming new relationships illustrates just how important it is to be **inclusive instead of exclusive**.

My brother Norm has a home on that same spot where my parent's cottage was. To this day our family migrates north to enjoy the bounty that Manistee Lake has to offer. It has always been and always will be a wellspring of love that gives my family an everlasting bond.

It Doesn't Add Up

Friends make everything better — we all know that. Summer gave way to fall so I had to leave the lake (kicking and screaming) and head back to school. The first day of high school is well… well… you know. Like most teenagers I was buzzing with anticipation and nearly sprang from my bed that morning; to me, high school was the 'big time'. I can honestly tell you it was one of the most intimidating days of my academic career. I was going from being a 'big fish in a small lake' to a guppy in a vast ocean. As many adults will attest to, at the age of 14 or 15 we think that we know everything and may think that we have what it takes to conquer the world. I didn't stand apart from that mindset, but I was in for a rude awakening when I passed through the arches of my high school.

I was the youngest of seven brothers and sisters so they had already made the scholastic leap from junior high, to high school and beyond. All of them had achieved honorable reputations in the process. By the time I stepped into my first classroom, many student circles were already referring to me as, 'the little sister'. I wanted to change the perception that I was 'the baby' of the family, so I began scouting for ways to set myself apart. At first, the task seemed overwhelming. Gary and Fred were incredible musicians and my other siblings were all gifted in their own right. Their popularity didn't help matters either; each time a new teacher referred to me I was accustomed to hearing, "Oh, you're the youngest LaCroix. You have a big family don't you?" This may not sound like a big deal, but after a few months of that treatment I became a little frustrated (some people even started calling me 'Cooney Babe' which was Fred's nickname). All I could do was roll with my new growing pains.

I thought, "I'm a pretty good student and I can hold my own as a musician. But I don't think I'm in the same class with my brothers and sisters when it comes to their talent. How am I going to stand out?"

The bell rang according to schedule and my new high school life was underway. I started by meandering through the halls to try and escape my family's shadows. As I turned a corner I saw my next classroom and realized how eager I was to reach the door: deep down I knew escaping the halls would make me forget about my worries. The strange thing was that the class I so eagerly looked forward to was algebra. Yes – algebra! I've always had a great affinity for math and enjoy the logic and structure of the mathematical process (nerd?). It was different from the music world but I knew that math would set me apart from my brothers and sisters.

The layout of the mathematics classroom was distinct and somewhat unconventional. My friends and I instantly thought it was the coolest way to set up a classroom. Unfortunately, what we didn't know was that our teacher laid out the tables that way for a particular reason. The tables were lined up three across and four deep (each sitting two students). During that first week each student was permitted to choose a seat. That luxury would come to a screeching halt because of the teacher's unorthodox rules.

The first morning our teacher walked into the room she appeared to be very rigid with her hair pulled back tightly from her classic wire-rimmed glasses. She started to call out the student's names and then she finally came to me...

In a condescending tone, she said, "Oh, you must be the baby of the La Croix family."

I said, "Yes, that's me."

The feeling I got from her was unsettling. Not only did I have to worry about passing the class, which other students labeled as 'grueling', but I had worries about how my teacher would perceive me based her knowledge of my siblings. My classmates and I were extremely dedicated to our studies because we were forewarned about random pop-quizzes that took place. It wasn't until I encountered that teacher that I started to doubt my mathematical capabilities. In my opinion, her hawkish and unrelenting ways were the very definition of 'poor' teaching. She came to the classroom everyday without the heart and passion that it takes to be a teacher who inspires students. On a Monday after one of her infamous pop-quizzes, a friend asked me how I did.

"I don't think I did all too well. I don't like how she teaches," I told my friend.

He said, "Well I hope you did alright because the teacher will start seating us according to our test scores this week!"

"What!" I yelled.

"Yeah... The teacher will sit the worst students in the front of class and the better students in the back. Be careful because she puts the worst student in the very front seat: in front of the entire class!"

Nervous and mortified, it was scary to think that I might have to sit in front of the class all by my lonesome. To picture myself perched up in front of all of my friends because I had received the lowest test score was crushing and demoralizing.

The day our teacher announced test scores, my nerves were shot. As I walked to class I was so apprehensive that I almost turned-tail and ran home. Then it came to me: the idea of how terrible it was for students to be subjected to that type of humiliation in a learning environment. I was lost in thought and as I sat down a panic stricken feeling came over me. She started by letting us know how disappointed she was with our scores and that we would now be sitting according to how well we did. She began to explain her seating arrangement according to scores. It was just her way of making a glaring example of the students who performed the worst; she felt that by sitting them closer to her they would perform better. I can't say that I agree with that.

One by one she rattled off the scores: Laurie, Mike, Nick, Kathy. The names kept coming, all but mine. My heart thumped as name after name passed and the seats filled up. There were only two chairs left, another student and I stood there as though we were the last two standing in her line of fire. Well, I was spared as I watched my friend head off to certain doom. The teacher singled him out and sat him down in the very first seat. I wasn't far behind. My teacher gave me her irreverent moody look of disappointment as she showed me to the second seat from the front. I wanted to crawl into a hole in order to escape the embarrassment.

I've never considered myself to be 'head-of-the-class' at any grade level; nor did I ever find myself hanging onto the bottom rung. My algebra teacher's approach to teaching had a negative effect on me in many ways. From the day our teacher sat me in that chair, my desire and drive to succeed in math began to run out of steam. She had taken the wind out of my sails, pulled alongside my ship and blasted a cannonball directly through the bow. I struggled and seldom made it out of the middle row as my math prowess became somewhat stagnant. To make matters worse, I learned I would have the same teacher for geometry the next year.

There was no doubt our teacher knew the subject matter front-to-back and around again. It was the condescending and passionless approach she taught with that caused many of her students to fail in grasping the fundamentals of algebra. Through her phlegmatic teaching, she lost my interest along with the rest of the class. She came to class with no passion and no desire to make a connection with the kids. As a result of watching her lethargic instruction, her students couldn't wait for the dust to settle and get out of that room. It was clear she didn't care one way or the other if students took a liking to the subject or not: it was truly a shame.

Although I can still remember that bad experience, it thrills me that our standards of teaching have evolved over the years. I highly doubt that a teacher of her caliber and passionless spirit could survive in today's school system. I advise teachers to just 'go for it'; to teach from the heart and with radiating energy. It is possible that teachers may never know the profound effect they have on every young mind they encounter.

I love hearing a story of a teacher's passion and conviction having such a great affect on students. The student carries that lesson throughout their life, in that; the teacher has turned learning into a gift. Show me a passionate teacher and I'll show you students who simply love to learn.

Better to Give

Who doesn't love Christmas? I have yet to meet someone who doesn't like the idea of ole St. Nick sliding down the chimney with presents in tow. Around the LaCroix house seeing fluffy white snow slowly filter down from the sky was like magic and only meant one thing: Christmas was coming! My family is Christian and we loved to show our gratitude when celebrating the birth of Christ. Here, I would like to stress that I believe we are given a freedom and spiritual calling to practice faith in any way we please. My family focused on the love that we wanted to give to others when we practiced our faith. Giving during the holiday season always brought immense joy and fulfillment to our household. This was our way of demonstrating to God the greatness we saw in humanity.

My parents firmly believed that x-mas was solely about giving… and give is what they most certainly did. Not only were my parents dedicated to giving to their family, but they also took the time to help the less fortunate. My family would gather up many presents so we could start to spread some great Christmas cheer. We spent Christmas Eve traveling around town visiting our neighbors, I can remember those days vividly. My eyes would open to a wonderland of crystal white snow that stretched for an eternity. Dad would already be dressed like Santa, ready to hit the road; but first, he had to wrangle up his elves (the reindeer were already outside, the Buick, that is). He called up to Fred, Gary and me to haul our butts downstairs to grab the gift bags. In our mechanical reindeer, we set out on our journey, sometimes the snow was so thick we could barely make out the roads. Fred would take the steering wheel because Santa had to tend to the presents in the back seat. It was always a blast watching dad bounce up and down like a bowl full of jelly as Fred put the pedal to the metal. Although the little gifts we passed out weren't expensive or extravagant (we gave out stockings filled with small toys and popcorn balls), the look of excitement and wonder on the faces of the children we visited left an indelible impression on me. To have such a positive effect on people who were a little less fortunate was a life changing experience. I learned that there is more gratification in giving than in receiving.

Santa and his elves spent the day sledding around in the snow. After we emptied all of the gift bags, we would make a direct line for a family member's house to spark up the Christmas celebration. The entire family would arrive and soon the place was rocking. One year Denny decided to assume the part of Santa Clause, giving my dad a well-deserved rest. Denny loved being Santa Clause. He also loved the idea of having a few 'drinks' to fuel his performance (cheer beer – if you will). He bent his elbow quite often on our Christmas Eve journey that year and by the time we were finished passing out the gifts he was feeling very "Christmassy".

That year our last stop was my sister Bernadette's house. Before we went into the house, Fred, Gary and I devised a small plan. For the kids' amusement we decided to go inside and act like we were waiting for Santa to arrive. So we all went in and got the kids excited for ole Saint Nick to come marching through the door. However, Santa didn't come in on cue so I began to worry. All of a sudden, we hear my nephew scream, "Mom! Mom! Look! Santa is peeing in the snow bank." My nephew Kenton spied my brother Denny, dressed from head-to-toe as St.

Nick, taking a whiz outside. We all let Denny know he was caught as we laughed and pointed from the window. I guess even Santa needs a pee-break now and then...

Those Christmas memories are priceless and my parents did everything they could to ensure it. They created a world so comfortable and joyous that I dare to remember a worry. A great thing about Christmas was celebrating our midnight mass where we would perform carols and musical sets for the congregation. It lasted long into the night that when we arrived home, we didn't have time to see our x-mass tree. We waited all night, usually without sleep, for the big morning to arrive. When Christmas time approached, my pulse pounded and my imagination exploded with thoughts of what might be downstairs. After my brothers and sisters woke up, my parents would have us all wait at the top of the stairs before we could come down to see the tree. When they opened the door to the living room we felt like we were whisked away into a fairy tale. Christmas music would be playing as we gazed upon the presents that lay beneath our beautiful tree. As I approached the neatly wrapped gifts, the inviting aroma of our majestic blue-spruce tree seemed to render me powerless as it drew me closer. The tree seemed to breathe life into the air that invigorated our Christmas spirit.

The Bass Queen

Every year during the first week of June, my home town was consumed by one of its most exciting events: "The Bass Festival". The entire community participated and the activities extended throughout the week. There were a few different components to the celebration. As the name "Bass Festival" may insinuate, the big time fisherman of the area dedicated themselves to their bass fishing craft. They competed for bragging rights to be called the best bass fisherman in the land. I was more concerned with another event that took place – the beauty pageant. Everyone in town recognized what a big deal the pageant was, to be chosen as the queen was an honor that remained on the tips of everyone's tongue the entire year.

The title, "Bass Queen", is certainly unique but I warn readers not to be disillusioned into thinking that it doesn't merit respect. As is common with any beauty pageant, looks certainly play a role in the outcome; however, I was more motivated by the talent portion. Looking to test my musical talents, I decided to focus on that part of the event. I was also motivated by the fact that I always thought my looks didn't measure up to those of the other girls in my town (I guess I suffered from the dreaded "ugly duckling" syndrome). I can remember feeling extremely anxious but also excited to compete for the crown.

I wanted to challenge myself to the fullest so I decided to write and perform my own songs. It was the first time I would be performing for a large crowd all by my lonesome. Up until that point of my musical career, I always had my family members to rely on for strong support. But this time was different; I would be alone on stage. If people's ears started to bleed I would have to face the firing squad all by myself. I didn't want to be unprepared for the big day so I spent months writing my songs and practiced them with great diligence. I honed my skills and aimed to become the big bass of the bunch.

Like any aspiring beauty Queen, I wanted to do everything in my power to make sure I was equipped to win. After practicing a great deal I felt confident that I could knock some socks off. The next course of action was to upgrade my physical appearance. I came up with the bright idea to sun bathe the day before the competition in hopes of finding a nice bronzing glow that would help me stand out. Unfortunately, I made the rookie mistake of falling asleep under the sun's bright rays. My tan didn't turn into a glorious bronze but rather a fire engine red. I use the word 'fire' because that's exactly how I felt, as though I was burning up. I guess it wasn't the sort of 'HOT' I was looking for. The next day I shook off the pain and headed to the pageant early to prepare. I started my warm ups and focused on the challenge that lay ahead.

Fear and anxiety began to rear its ugly head. As the seconds ticked down before my performance, I realized I needed to put my money where my mouth was (for that large-mouth bass crown). I would be on display for everyone to pick apart and judge: the nerves were kicking in. The contest was a great measuring stick to gauge my talents and I wanted to use it to help me decided if I should attend college for vocal studies. I realized that if I wanted to get serious about accomplishing that goal, I must conquer the pageant and prove to myself that I had the musical chops to do so.

The decisive moment arrived and I found myself on stage in a small chair. I was only equipped with my guitar and my voice; it was time to get serious. The spotlight hit my eyes as I began to sing, I can honestly say that was one the most nervous moments of my life. I can remember not being able to feel my fingers as I played my guitar — I was utterly trembling. Halfway through my performance I knew I had to trump my fear.

I said to myself, "Give it all you've got girl, there is no turning back now."

In all of my sunburned glory I belted out my songs just as I had practiced them and before I could blink my performance was over. It seemed like time stood still as I looked out over the audience in anticipation of their reaction. They let out a warm and raucous cheer; I couldn't believe it, they loved my performance. The reaction to my music was absolutely exhilarating. After soaking up the sounds of my town's approval, I took a modest bow and then sauntered off stage.

The other girls competing against me were extremely talented. One by one they all made their way to the stage and wowed the crowd. They all had their own unique twist and each of them seemed to shine like stars. I knew that winning the crown wasn't going to be easy. I remember feeling such apprehension when the final girl was done performing, I didn't know what the judges had in store for us. My heart sank as the judge made his way to the stage to announce the winners. The winner of the talent portion was to be called first – when I heard him call my name as the winner, I almost jumped out of my sun-laden skin. I felt like I was floating and couldn't believe it! Next, the judge would announce the runners-up for ultimate prize, the crown of the Bass Queen. I remember hoping that my name would ring out sooner or later. The third place qualifier was selected and then the first runner up was called out, my name wasn't called so my hopes began to sink. Suddenly, my name rang out! I was chosen as the winner and the new reigning Bass Queen. I stood there paralyzed in utter shock and couldn't believe that I had risen to the occasion. Then it sunk in: I realized the Bass Queen crown was now mine!

That experience taught me many things: not only did it help me access my musical skills, but it taught me how I reacted to pressure. Gaining that newfound knowledge was so important because it helped to adjust my future plans in regards to my musical life. The critical lesson I learned that day was this: although life may be going in one definite direction, our choices and God given destiny have the uncanny knack of altering everything.

What I Have Gained

My youth was filled with love in my little bedroom (the closet). It constantly reminded me 'to love my surroundings'. Appreciating what we have, will grant us the freedom to feel good about our life no matter where we land. I have learned that God grants each of us with our own unique blessings for the sole purpose of designing our lives.

My first steps – taught me about the critical ideology of *'failing forward'*. Even when we are pressed down with a weight so heavy that we feel our backs may break, focusing on the positive usually will dissipate any negative that may come from the task. I've learned that we've already failed if we haven't begun to try.

To proceed with *honesty* will help us bear fruit and succeed: without honesty, we have already failed. A simple sparkling red apple taught me the *'value of honesty'*. When I took the apple and claimed it as my own – for me I knew I was wrong; being dishonest can only haunt us with guilt and provide us with desperate, empty lives. Through truth we obtain greater enrichment, as many doors will swing wide open for new wonderful adventures.

Spending summers at the lake provided me with the incredible opportunity to *'be inclusive instead of exclusive'*. I accepted everyone over the years and made many great friends by loving everyone's **uniqueness**. By learning acceptance of our differences, I was able to become familiar with so much of a world outside of my own.

Through it all, I tried to live with conscious passion. Passion plays a majority role in life and often lends to who we are and how we either infect or positively affect the world. To teach, to play, to love, to communicate – to do these things with stinging passion can only favor and enrich our lives. *Passion creates love and love heals.*

The quickest road to passion and love is through *'giving'*. When we give... love is felt. Whether it's through inanimate objects or a piece of our soul, we are creating love and connection to those who surround us.

Those were just a few of the things I've gained early in life. As you read further you will see how my carefully constructed choices led me to the adventurous steps along my path.

End of ACTS I.

INNER MISSIONS

The following missions are my personal values from ACTS I that I embrace.

Acceptance: Accept everyone's Uniqueness as Perfection

Choices:

- o Appreciate My Surroundings

- o Fail Forward

- o Have Faith

- o Be Inclusive Instead of Exclusive

- o Have Passion

- o Have Humor

Truth: Be honest at all times

Sharing: Give loving support to others

ACTS
PART II

Monumental Choices

At the age of eighteen I was confronted with a decision that would affect the rest of my life: whether to get married or go to college. Instead of spreading my wings and taking flight to college I decided to get married. At the time I was in love and that's what ultimately took precedence in my choice. We're all confronted with life changing decisions that when we look back, we might think of how we could have done things differently.

Although my marriage ended after 11 years I would wholeheartedly make the decision to get married again. Through telling this story I'd like to prove that if a marriage doesn't hold up it's not a failure, not at all. My first marriage gave me two of my most prized gifts, my first two sons: Nathan and Dean. They are my pride and joy. Every time I speak about them I become the classic loving mother with wide grateful eyes. That marriage also blessed me with great in-laws who were always kind and loving with my family. It's because of how strong our relationship has grown over the years that I think of my mother and father-in-law as a second set of parents. You'll never hear me utter the phrase, "Oh God, the in-laws are here!"

Doctors believed that I wouldn't be able to have children, but at the age of 22, I learned that I was pregnant with my first son Nathan (with a name like Mary, I guess it was God's will to have me conceive). I remember the shock and surprise when I heard the news and when I held my baby for the first time: I was mesmerized. My husband and I now had a little life that was completely dependent on us. The idea gave new meaning to the word 'responsibility'. I loved being a new mom and the bonding experience that came along with it. I especially cherished feeding my little guy during quiet nights while he wrapped his little hand around my finger with such strength that he seemed he would never let go. It so touched my heart. This beautiful baby could have had just about anything his heart desired, because he instantly had mine.

Before my pregnancy I worked at the county courthouse in the accounts payable/receivables department. After several months as a stay at home mom I decided to go back to work. Shortly after my return (and after some hard work) I was promoted to a new position that involved overseeing the payroll and benefits division. The division consisted of 12 unions that were made up of approximately 1,500 employees. I became involved in negotiating contracts with the unions and learned how to work productively with a variety of people. Needless to say, it was a demanding job but the overall professional experience I gained helped me lay a solid foundation for what was to become my business career. The experience the position granted me allowed a person without a college degree to become successful in the business world. Yes, I do say it here and now that it's possible to obtain your life's ambitions without a 'formal college education'. I'm living and breathing proof of it.

Although I chose marriage over school, I believe that nowadays, more often than ever, a college degree is essential to a young person's success (the business paradigm has obviously changed over the years). Unfortunately, I've learned that colleges often lack the courses that teach 'real world' business experiences. It's a tricky subject, some say the only way to learn is by doing.

The question is, how can a student learn the hardedge side of the business world in a classroom setting?

I stress that teaching young students how to apply their knowledge in real situations is detrimental to one's career development. I've decided to speak about the professional world as well as the spiritual, in hopes of helping individuals understand there are an abundant number of pathways that can lead to success in both.

After several years of cranking away in the business world, Dean (my second son) came knocking. God had blessed me with a second child. Dean has always been filled with great energy that spills over into his work ethic. He is tireless in his pursuits and exudes intelligence (he certainly kept my husband and me extremely busy, darting around the house like a wild little mongoose). Although my husband and I loved our boys, we encountered certain marital strains over the 11 years we spent together. Divorce seemed to be the amicable solution to our problem so we separated. I found myself alone and supporting two young boys: I was in for an interesting ride. After taking a short maternity leave to have Dean, I returned to my municipal job but the income wasn't nearly enough to properly support a family of three. As I've said, there are many paths in life to explore in order to succeed. That was exactly what I was about to do.

I decided to take a real estate course and begin to sell homes while still working for the municipality. I took to 'sales' like a bee to honey, I loved laying down a good sales pitch and interacting with bright-eyed, prospective homeowners. Real estate wasn't the greatest industry to get involved with because mortgage interest-rates were approximately 14% at the time. I refused to let the negative tides of influence get to me, so after hard work (and growing pains) in the real estate industry I managed to become pretty successful. During that stage of my career I realized that by merging my sales and benefits experience, I could create a new professional business tool. A new weapon if you will. I knew my experience, if used correctly, could and would lead to new opportunities. I gave it a shot and combined my skill-sets in sales and benefits administration into one little neatly packaged portfolio: Me. That new approach quickly paid off when I landed a new job with a very lucrative managed healthcare company. My new mission: selling health benefits to major corporations.

I must say that managing two boys and a healthy workload wasn't the easiest time of my life. When the pressures and responsibilities became too much for me to bear I didn't dwell on the negative. I decided to get things done by attacking my daily routine with a soldier's veracity. Driving through those challenges wouldn't have been possible without help from family. My niece, Lori, is one of the blessed souls who came to my rescue to help me through some rough times. She was an angel and quickly became part of our immediate family (thankfully, she agreed to move in with us). What a God send she was. Lori played a major role in my family's daily life and I often referred to her as the 'engine' that helped our family dynamic. She became part of the family and most of all Lori became one of my best friends. Her friendship is what I valued most. As my career became more and more demanding I would lean on Lori more often; not only for help around the house but for moral support as well. Without her love, my household would have turned into a circus with me trying to be the ringmaster.

With my career in full swing and the house in order (most of the time), I felt extremely blessed that things were going well. Life got even better when I was given the opportunity to work fulltime with one organization and that meant that I only had to work one job! Just the thought of simplifying my life was exhilarating. The only question that lingered in the back of my mind was if the position would grant me the financial stability to properly provide for my family. After I learned that it paid roughly 40k a year, I was elated and felt secure in that I could support my family in the way that I needed to.

My new job fit me well, so well in fact that going to the office didn't feel like a chore but a privilege. It motivated me to push a little harder and after a couple years of working my nimble fingers to the bone, I began to get some attention. Attention that got me promoted to Regional Sales Manager. I was honored and grateful for the confidence my colleagues had shown in me. With that new job came a new challenge, it was a position so demanding that the person brave enough to take it would either sink like a brick or learn to swim with the sharks. I put doubt and fear aside and trusted that God would help me overcome obstacles that were sure to come my way.

A fresh new job in an exciting environment can give someone great opportunities in many areas of the business world. Technology, interesting co-workers, and travel were all things I looked forward to. That new position is where I met my second husband. First, we got to know each other as colleagues and then we became involved on a personal level. We established a great friendship and decided to get married. A few months later I learned I would be having my third child (so much for not being able to have children). We decided to name this new angel, "W". You read that correctly, "W" is actually my son's first name. At the time it was considered a 'signature name' and un-surprisingly the name is still very unique amongst his friends today. Over the years W has realized that it's easier to not have to explain his name – now he goes by Blake (which is his middle name). He has become the standout musician and has been blessed with my father's exceptional musical talent. W continues to develop his craft to this day.

When I got back to work after maternity leave it was business as usual. Before I could even set my bag down at my desk the work started to come in. Immediately, I felt like a cashew in a can of mixed nuts. Not only was I getting back into the swing of things but I had to adjust to some new developments. Unfortunately, before my maternity leave, I entrusted my responsibilities to one of my staff members who began jockeying for my position and tried to 'squeeze me out'. The news shocked me and struck a personal cord within. I was especially hurt because I was the person who hired and gave the employee opportunities to excel. When you hear that business can be 'cut-throat', it's not a lie.

I thought, "How could they possibly replace me with the person I hired -- especially during maternity leave?" I was headstrong and didn't take the situation lightly. As I thought about the actions of my employee I realized she crossed certain boundaries and I knew we had entered into unethical waters. There was only one choice for me to make and it was a drastic one. Ultimately, I suggested that she leave the company.

It was a difficult thing. My staff and I had become close, so the aftereffects of her departure weren't pleasant. Since that time I've grown in both my professional and personal life. If given that same choice, whether or not to keep an employee like that, I feel I would have handled the situation differently. The person I am today would have tried to work out a better solution to the problem. If I realized how important the position was to that person, I certainly would have done everything in my power to arrive at an amicable end. That unpleasant business scenario was painful; however, it was detrimental for me to learn how to deal with those difficult decisions. That experience helped me develop into a successful manager. I learned first-hand: what doesn't kill you can make you stronger.

That challenging managerial episode motivated me to seek out other opportunities in the business industry. Fortunately I had learned so much about my profession from playing an integral role in the managed health care industry that it made it easier to research opportunities elsewhere. I decided to learn everything I could about my field and hopefully kick down a door or two. First, I took a look at the prescription drug industry's major cost components and tried to determine if I could affect the market in any way (I know – a daunting idea). After I learned of the industry's rapidly accelerating costs, I was compelled to sink my teeth into the problem to bring about change. To do so, I found a company whose primary focus was managing prescription drug benefits. My goal was clear: I wanted to become an invaluable piece of that company's infrastructure in order to make a difference. My path was set.

Seeing as how I had three children and changed jobs so rapidly during those years, one may ascertain that my life was a little chaotic. I can say they weren't because I continued to be vigilant and didn't waiver from my plan. Constructing a well thought out road map to life is an important ingredient to becoming successful. It's also essential to know that a plan alone isn't the critical element for success: to actually believe in the plan is. By taking it one step at a time, without distraction or insecurity (add dash of flexibility), a person has the power to achieve their goals.

During that chaotic time of my life I was consciously planning and designing my career path. I used my own method to develop an education in both business and life that worked for me. I couldn't have accomplished certain things without the generosity, wisdom and guidance from the people that surrounded me. It's crucial to learn from your experiences, but it's wise to eagerly learn from anyone who is willing to take the time to act as a teacher. I recognize that God placed countless fascinating people in my life who were willing to act as mentors. I used my experiences, some brute strength and a dash of confidence to reach the next step of my professional design.

What was the next step? Well –without having a job lined up or any possibilities on the horizon I gave notice that I would be leaving my beloved company. It may not have been the wisest decision at the time because it went against my business protocol. I decided to trust in myself and take a divine leap of faith. It was an easy choice and almost organic. I believed God would be by my side to provide me the strength that I needed to take on each new step of my path.

Oh By the Way, Never Give Up

Without a secure job lined up I was quickly forced to establish a good relationship with an executive employment search firm: the grueling and very exhausting interview process was about to take off. After several intense meetings, I met an engaging CEO of a prescription drug company, one that I had researched. He and I hit it off and after many interviews a good feeling began to brew. I was sure an offer was on the horizon but to my dismay another applicant was given the job. The disappointment was magnified ten-fold due to the fact that I had been out of work for nearly nine months! Financially, life wasn't filled with roses and certainly wasn't filled with the frilly things we sometimes take for granted. All I could do was move forward and continue my quest by putting one brave foot in front of the next. My options were few and my prospects were dwindling.

I decided that staying in the 'professional loop' was the best thing to do. At the time it was my intention to let that CEO know that I was always willing to work. Periodic phone calls and simple 'how are you doing' interactions were my way of keeping in touch with him. Time passed but I refused to waiver and after about three weeks my persistence paid off. The CEO called to inform me his original hire didn't work out and that the position was mine if I wanted it! However, there were a few change-ups in the initial offering. The job no longer garnered the title of 'Director', but was downgraded to a managerial position. Also, the salary and benefits package would be less than what we originally discussed. I didn't blink an eye as I accepted the job offer with light in my heart. At that moment I can actually remember feeling my feet touching down on my path as a new world of business was now open to free exploration.

Infinite opportunities were afoot and after a week I was settling into my new digs just nicely. One thing I always knew to be true when entering a new office environment was that making friends and gaining the trust of one's staff is critical. Luckily, I was blessed with a dream team that made my adjustment not only easy, but fun. They were a great bunch of individuals who from day one helped me tackle the innumerable responsibilities the position came with. I was responsible for sales, account management, public relations, marketing and labor relations. At times my job was overwhelming and I felt as though I was in a pressure cooker that was about to blow sky-high. Needless to say, there was an intense amount of stress; but the stress was out-weighed by my appreciation for the challenge.

On a beautiful crystal clear day our CEO requested me for a quick 'catch-up' chat. He asked me how I was finding my way and how things were going (of course things were great). Then like many fast talking CEOs are prone to do, he said, "Oh by the way, I'm not sure if you know but we're in the process of making the transition to a new mainframe platform. The complete transition will take about six weeks and you are responsible for the part that needs to happen within a two-week period. This will all take place within three months." He continued, "Oh by the way – we have about 1,500 clients on file so you and your staff are responsible for transferring all of their information to the new system, mainly by hand. Just so you know, we're not able to have a 'tandem' system transfer, so when we flip the switch to transfer everything to the new system, there's no turning back".

"Oh my, do you know what this means?" I asked.

Firmly, he said, "I most certainly do so you better start working on your plan right now."

I walked out of that office with my head on a swivel; it was the first time in my career of being faced with such a grandiose task. My team would have to shine and strongly rely on each other to conquer the new mission (and **conquer** is exactly what we did). My team and I worked seamlessly as a well-oiled machine that battered down any and all obstacles that sprung up. We were excited and felt we had accomplished something substantial, something to be proud of. I can remember wanting to take a quick second to breathe, but then I heard our CEO call out, "Oh by the way (that was his catch-phrase and ultimately my sub-title), over the next 90 days we'll be working on the following objectives. First, we'll aim to win the business of several large corporations. You'll also be responsible for the integration of staff from the companies that we are about to acquire. Also, within the next six months we'll be taking our company through an initial public offering on the NASDAQ."

That influx of information and new responsibility was nothing short of a cyclonic business tornado. I also learned that the ultimate plan was to grow our company's worth, quickly, from 50 million dollars in revenue to a half billion dollars (I realized why the previous applicant bowed out of the job). I wasn't sure how to approach the endless list of things screaming through my mind; I really felt like going to the ladies room and throwing up (but I knew that wouldn't be the best executive decision). I shrugged off the fear and after some deliberation with my sparkling staff we laid out a bulletproof plan.

It was no secret that my performance and that of my team would ultimately determine the strength of our IPO. As I mentioned, one of our herculean tasks was the integration of employees from companies we acquired into our business environment. Executing that part of my job required extensive travel. A trip took me to Pennsylvania for a visit with one of the companies we were acquiring and the goal was to meet their sales team to provide them with the details of the integration. It was one of my first major business presentations so when I stepped in front of their sales people, I felt like I was on stage. Things were going well when shortly into my presentation a beautiful young woman with platinum hair raised her hand and stopped me dead in my tracks.

"Did I hear you say that your company was acquiring ours?" she asked.

I quickly realized that none of the employees had been informed about the impending acquisition (this was all happening with their CEO in the room). All I could think of was how to get myself out of that unnerving situation as quickly as possible. I looked around the table as the people waited with baited breath, eager for an answer.

"I think we need a quick break, please excuse us for a bit," I said as I glanced at their CEO (we went to a separate room as he was accompanied by his attorney).

"What the heck is going on?" I asked as I held back an impending eruption.

He said, "Well, there were some last minute problems with the negotiations. Everything was supposed to be finalized before today; however, I decided to not call the meeting off. I told our staff that we were only doing a joint venture instead of being acquired."

"What are you talking about?" Why wasn't I told?" I asked.

Timidly, he said, "We thought you were informed. I'm letting you know that things have been ironed out and will be going through as planned."

After our quick side-chat the meeting reconvened. Their CEO finally informed his employees of the company's impending sale. I stood next to him and could feel the contempt and puzzlement from the people who worked so hard for that company. Unfortunately, those squeamish situations arise from time-to-time, so it's crucial to learn how to adapt on the fly. For me, I had to learn a difficult lesson then and there in front of those hard working people. The following weeks saw the acquisition go smoothly as my team and I worked diligently on integrating the new staff — the platinum blonde woman who challenged me in the meeting became one of our best employees, her name was Krista. She and I established a great business and personal relationship over the years and had many exciting business adventures together. We are still great friends and that day in Pennsylvania is still etched in my business mind. I still think of that day with mixed emotions, fortunately, I pushed through the adversity and accomplished my team's goals. With hard work comes reward. Our diligence paid off when the IPO proved to be a success. I felt we all made great contributions that bolstered our company's progression.

My career was really starting to come together; however, at home things weren't paying off like the IPO was. My husband and I couldn't smooth out some rocky situations so we decided to separate and then ultimately divorce. My divorce added unwanted stress onto a heap of already simmering emotions. I shrugged it off and kept plugging away and made certain to stick to my path; I decided to put aside my personal turmoil to focus on my career. After climbing mountains of hard work and dedication I was promoted to Vice President of Sales: That was an incredible milestone for me (one I didn't think possible). When that day came, as you can guess, I thought I had reached the summit of Mt. Everest. But stop – not so fast. It was more like being at base camp staring up at a slope of infinite challenges.

Climbing Mountains

There I was, sitting at base camp with a new title. From that position there was only one direction to go: up! The next order of business was to try and secure one of the largest accounts in the prescription benefit world. I was on a team of four that would present to that company's panel who would ultimately decide whether or not to use our company's resources. The presentation was going smoothly and around noon we all broke for lunch. During that time the executive vice president of our parent company was suddenly called away. He returned a while later and informed us that the client had made a critical decision. Whomever they awarded the business must have an employee who was willing to relocate. That employee would have to work on-site with the client in their home state. He then said they wanted an answer that very same day so as to make a final decision on who would be awarded the business. Additionally, we were informed that the prospective client was strongly suggesting me for the assignment.

"Mary, would you move if we are awarded the account?" the executive vice president of our parent company asked me.

I couldn't believe that he was actually asking me to uproot my life and move to a different state (I had often mentioned that relocation wasn't in my plans). There was no way I was moving. My oldest son was only a junior in high school so I certainly didn't want to move him from his life at that particular time.

I boldly said, "No. I don't want to move. Look, for the time being can't we just tell them that we'll put together a team that will meet their expectations?"

"That's fine. We'll give it a shot," he answered.

The rest of the presentation went smoothly and afterwards a question and answer segment began. We were asked by the panel, "Have you all decided who the account representative will be – the one who will be relocating?"

My boss and CEO stood and said, "Yes, we have. Mary said she would take the job and move whenever necessary."

I was mortified and felt frozen with shock: he had flat out misled them. The meeting came to a close and I found it hard to find any words to express how I felt. Misleading people went against everything I believed in; being honest and true to others no matter how difficult the situation may be is how I live my life.

On the flight home I sat motionless in my seat next to my business partner. We both were silent for a great time and then he turned to me and asked, "Mary you're gone aren't you?" I couldn't muster up a response as my eyes began to swell with tears. Without saying anything he knew that I was already planning to leave the company I so dearly loved.

Our team had certainly achieved a lot and reached so many milestones, but it seemed tainted after that meeting. I returned home, choosing to stay under the radar for a while.

After a few weeks, my team received news that we got the account and immediately I knew what I had to do. I chose to leave the company because of our differences and it was without a doubt one of the most painful decisions I've ever made. I was so grateful for my incredible staff that had become like family to me and I knew it would be a gut-wrenching time saying goodbye. That experience made me a believer that it's possible to be friends with one's co-workers that you are responsible for. Sometimes that is the only way.

Making that choice to venture back out into the workforce was a life changing decision. I realized I was in the midst of a major change and the immediate decisions that I made would affect my family's life forever. Fortunately, a few weeks prior, an executive recruiter made contact with me. He asked if I would be interested in a potential employment opportunity with one of his clients, that client was looking for a vice president of account management. The recruiter had contacted me again and informed me he was looking for a referral for someone to fill that vice president position we had actually discussed. When I heard him mention that the job was still open I thought it must have been a sign from God. There I was in my frazzled state and beside myself with worry… and then the phone rang with incredible news. I quickly told him that I had a change of heart and asked if he could keep me in mind for the job. I felt that it could be the path I was meant to take and as fate would have it, the interview was on.

The Pinnacle of a Career

Before the interview that was perhaps the most important of my career, I remember feeling like a child just beginning to walk as butterflies nervously fluttered throughout my stomach. Although nervous, I reminded myself of one irrefutable fact: that I had nothing to lose and everything to gain. With no glaring consequences, the job was mine for the taking. I kept reassuring myself that I would be perfect for the position. The recruiter informed me that they were looking for someone that not only had the experience that I had, but also wanted someone with connections to the labor side of our business. My many years working with unions had turned into a significant plus. As I stepped into the office I decided to look at my interviewers not as a firing squad, but as engaging conversationalists. I wanted the job but also wanted to make sure that the company and I would dance together nicely. So I asked some questions of my own. The questions bounced around the room like super balls and the more I asked, the more the interviewers became the interviewees. The tone of the conversation transformed into an easy going banter that allowed everyone to speak freely. That particular interview illustrated to me just how valuable communication skills are in one's professional development.

The conversation with my interviewers paid off as I was awarded the position (my apprehensive heart skipped a beat). The next pivotal task that lay ahead was informing my current employer that I would be leaving the company; he was understandably surprised when I told him.

"Why are you leaving?" he asked.

I answered the best I could. "Well, as you already know when you stood in-front of those people and said I would move you broke some major rules that I follow: rules that I live by. I've always been 'up-front' with people no matter what the case may be. What makes matters worse is that those people trusted me and I feel you've broken that trust."

I swiftly gave my two weeks notice in the most graceful way I could think of. After which, some suspicious activity on my boss's part began to catch my eye. I realized he didn't want to magnify the situation (I thought it was because of the way he had misled the customer). Perhaps the most surprising part of me leaving the company was the fact my boss never once asked who I intended to work for next.

My departure was final and I was back into a sea of new business ventures. After setting up shop in my new office I was astounded by the phone calls that started to roll in from former co-workers of mine. They explained to me that they were looking for new opportunities and just couldn't stay trapped in the old company any longer. One friend who was most interested in a change of scenery was Krista, the sharp platinum blonde I had befriended. Krista and another close associate explained that it was their time to leave that company so I informed them of incredible opportunities that were on the horizon. They expressed their interest and we set a plan in motion. We all stayed true to each other and soon found ourselves back on the same team.

The first order of business for us was to master the installation of prescription benefits for a monstrous automotive conglomerate (one of the biggest players in the game). The job was daunting and at times overwhelming, but Krista was our secret weapon. Our 'ace in the hole' had worked closely with similar companies; she knew the process well. Krista's knowledge was priceless and with each member of the team stepping up perfectly, the project was a huge success. However, unforeseen problems were stirring and gaining strength out in the volatile prescription benefit world.

A massive and ugly legal storm was brewing all right. I learned that my former employer was hitting me, personally, with a multimillion-dollar lawsuit. The basis of the lawsuit stipulated that there was a 'non-compete' clause involved in the contract I had with them. That meaning my previous employer didn't want me to work for anyone who could be considered competition. But as it was, the two companies were exactly that, major rivals in the prescription drug industry so my previous employer was looking to cause some legal friction. The serious nature of the accusations, to put it bluntly, scared the *hebegebees* out of me. For starters, I wasn't sure how my managers would react to the news (it's not every day that you're confronted with a huge lawsuit). I knew my job could be hanging by a thread so I was on edge, a razor's edge that could split my world into two. A 'talk' was scheduled between the heads of my new company and me to discuss the situation. As I made my way to their office all I could do was trust in the fact that I had done nothing wrong and God would see me through. I was put at ease when our company's legal team said they would support me in any and all matters that might arise. My supportive company planned to bring in a savvy team of attorneys to impose a counter suit against my former employer.

My heart decided against going into an arrhythmia as I sat back in my chair. After months of preparing for a huge legal battle, to our surprise, my previous employer decided to drop the suit entirely! After some time passed and I decompressed from that unwanted anxiety, it came to light that the suit was only meant to deter me from taking a major client away from them. That major account was detrimental if they wanted to be acquired in the future.

Over the next year my company and I made certain not to cross any ethical lines and to stay clear of any more legal obstacles. We worked diligently and over time won the business of the client that my previous employer was afraid we would win. The business world is a mixture of complicated interwoven puzzles to solve and for my team we could honestly say – all's well that ended well.

My new division was now managing approximately 4½ billion dollars worth of business. The demanding work schedule was tireless but rewarding on so many levels. Although the idea of travel and leaving my boys didn't sit well with me, it was ultimately part of the program. During my first year on the job I commuted from Detroit to New Jersey every week so the travel was becoming routine and my boys were getting comfortable with it. Then, out of nowhere, I was asked to move to our company's headquarters in Chicago: at the time I loved the idea. My oldest son Nathan had graduated form high school by then and was in college. The fact that my company respected me enough as well to ask and work through it with me was another reason why I embraced the idea. I loved Chicago and felt it was the right time for a move so the plan was set in motion. My two sons, Krista, my business team and I packed our bags and headed off to start a brand new life.

Chicago is a city that has secured a warm, cozy place in my heart. When my dedicated and scrappy team arrived we found that the city was a place where anything was possible. That move cemented the idea that combining my skills had paid off; the avenues intersected seamlessly and life was surrounded with a brilliant glow in the windy city. I had truly reached the pinnacle of my career. After three years passed things were going smoothly in the windy city. Wait, did I say smoothly?

Work was great, however, there was one glaring aspect (or thorn in my side) that just wouldn't go away. The more grueling my work schedule became the more I found myself separated from my sons. I spent more time in the air than I did on the ground and did all I could to balance work and family life. That balance came to an abrupt end when I was pulled away from a meeting in New Jersey. I was informed that my son, Dean, had been involved in an accident at school back in Chicago. Frantically I tried calling the school and after some cleaning up some heavy beads of sweat, I finally got in touch with the school nurse.

The nurse's distant voice rang out, "I think your son has broken his arm and we need you to come in to give us permission to administer the proper care."

Needless to say, my worries were alleviated when I knew Dean would be just fine. With that episode behind me and after my business affairs were sealed up, I hopped on the next flight and headed for home. It was then that my conscience started to play with my.... conscience. What if something catastrophic had happened while I was away? What if my sons needed me and I couldn't get to them?

To be honest I felt ashamed and neglectful for not thinking of those scenarios until that very moment. Worst of all, I hadn't prepared for anything of the sort. I reached up to turn on the over-head light to get some reading done. In that very moment, I decided to redesign my life and schedule it so that I could be closer to my sons. Perhaps that overhead light that shined so brightly into my eyes made me understand what I was missing at home. I knew it was time to make the changes necessary so that I could care for my children in every way I wanted.

It's Time to Change

By redesigning my schedule I was able to spend more quality time with my boys and although I was extremely happy with the choice, there was something bubbling just beneath the surface. I surprised everyone when I made the decision to change career paths yet again. People were shocked because I appeared to be cruising along nicely. I was making nearly seven figures and could actually say that I was happy with the work I was doing. After explaining the fact that I wanted to redesign my life to be closer to my kids, my close friends and family expressed their concerns for what I was about to do.

About a year earlier I was contacted by an executive recruiter about job opportunities so I decided to test the waters again by casting my line back out to sea. I gave him a call to touch base with the intention of decreasing my business travel obligations. The recruiter let me know that a CEO of a telecommunications company in Denver was searching for a vice president to develop his company's healthcare division. We set up an interview and when I met the man I was impressed by his energy and enthusiasm as we easily struck up conversation. By the end of the interview I had heard enough and was interested in the job. I thoroughly illustrated how important it was to be close to my boys without the burden of sporadic travel; fortunately, the news didn't deter him from hiring me. As fate would have it, the CEO let me know he owned a private jet that could make life a lot easier in my business travels. Obviously, that bit of information sparked my interested. Honestly, I didn't think he would pursue me for the job (I wasn't particularly interested in moving to Denver so I was comfortable with any decision).

The Gods must have been smiling because the vibrant CEO decided to hire me. He assured me that the travel would be light and there was only one big request: that I sign a one year contract with the company. During that one year commitment I would be responsible for two major objectives: one, setting up a solid healthcare division and the other was to bring in new contracts. I committed to his terms and was sure to keep my 'non-compete' part of the contract in mind (that was trouble that I didn't want any part of again). The deal was done so my kids and I spent the summer in Chicago preparing for the next chapter of our lives, moving to Denver. Planning for the move raised the chaos level in our house from moderate to intense. We were on the move and it was all happening so fast. One major priority of mine was finding a comfortable house to move into. Fortunately, I found a lovely 6,000 square foot home at the foothills of the Rocky Mountains. After settling in I can remember my boys and I sitting back and thinking that we had landed in God's country.

Heading into work that first day I felt like a kid on her first day of school – anxiously anticipating new and interesting challenges that lay ahead. I was especially excited to meet my incredible new staff and that's exactly what they proved to be: 100% incredible. As a team we accomplished a boatload of tasks and leaped over substantial obstacles that came our way. Although I sensed the feeling of accomplishment swirling within us all, something continued to loom heavily over my head. It was my desire to spend even more time with my sons and they felt the same way.

After dedicating a solid 14 months to my work and staying true to my contractual agreements, I made the difficult decision to resign from my job and leave the company altogether. I gave my two weeks notice and focused on the plan that I'd been setting up for some time: next stop Sarasota, FL. Florida is home to many of my family members so I felt the decision was wise because we would all have the chance to be closer. Two of my closest relatives, my brother and his wife, loved the thought of us all living in the same town. I also had some business ideas as I planned on starting my own healthcare consulting firm while living on the coast. I moved forward by investing money in the company and hired several employees (I was fortunate to have a ready-made client base). Those who were on board were extremely driven and excited for the new opportunities on the horizon: things were sunny and promising. Somehow during that whirlwind, I secured my Florida real-estate license with an agency working out of Sarasota. My plate was overflowing with projects, objectives and responsibility. You name it and I probably was involved in it. Although I felt swamped at times, I completely loved life and so did my boys.

Working for all of those years in the managed healthcare industry taught me many things.

One glaring lesson I learned was that the industry is turbulent and always transforming. As we were building our business in Florida the economy went into crisis and forced many of our clients to default on their bills – which ultimately resulted in them filing for bankruptcy. The seas got rough and the business world became unforgiving. After nearly three years of grinding the stone to make things work, the industry's downturn resulted in me losing a significant portion of the money I had invested. After a few other thorns were lodged into my delicate side we couldn't keep the company afloat; in time we had to close up shop. It was unfortunate but I always take valuable lessons away from my experiences and that particular time taught me to hang-tough no matter how hard the torrential hurricane winds may blow. I was facing some of the hardest times of my life and in the distance, a place called *paradise* beckoned.

What I Have Gained

Perhaps the most important lessons I've learned is *'to know myself'*. How can we make well informed and educated decisions unless we truly make choices that represent what we are? I've always tried to stand for something – my professional life taught me a lot about how to stand up for truth and my belief in others.

My career in business was frantic at best and often times it was impossible to keep up with the chaotic juggling act. Through the career maze I learned one special thing: to introduce balance into my life in order to make things work more smoothly. That balance, after some hardships and tough times, allowed me to live a more fulfilled life with my family and friends. To know yourself and what you stand for will ultimately lead to a balanced world that you can take significant pride in.

End of ACT II.

INNER MISSIONS

The following missions are personal goals from ACTS II that I aim to embrace.

Acceptance: Always forgive no matter what the situation or condition.

Choices:

- o Always work to create new business opportunities.

- o Stay close to my loving family.

Truth: Make choices that represent who I am through tactful honesty.

Sharing: Mentor others while allowing others to mentor me.

ACTS
PART III

Just Like Moving to Paradise

There is an area of Florida that rivals my most dream-like idea of what 'Paradise' might be like. Whimsical – pristine – God-fairing: I've discovered a land, a 'down-home' town that has seeped into my soul. This maze of kindness is inhabited by some of the friendliest human beings I have ever met.

After weathering those turbulent years on the sandy beaches of Sarasota, I found myself on the move again. My decision to relocate to paradise was fueled by my desire to reconnect with nearly forty family members who lived in 'Paradise'. During that time, I realized that being around my family was the best option; not only for me but for my boys. My amazing family would be there to support me all the while lending their open hearts whenever I needed.

When I touched down in paradise I secured a position as a design sales person in a furniture store: that meant I was entering a new professional era. The job was completely foreign to me; which in turn stirred up an excitement that I loved immediately. I was in a new career and with all new positions come the necessary training regimens. My employer informed me of the three-month training program that was ahead and during that time of training I would receive an hourly wage. After several years of owning my own company I then had to think in different terms when it came to my personal finance. I convinced myself to think that the word 'salary' had only one meaning; a vegetable. The change was somewhat shocking but I was willing to welcome any and all financial opportunities.

The day I received my first paycheck, a course of exhilaration ran from the tips of my toes to the excitement in my eyes. The idea of being paid by an employer was far more comforting to me than getting stuck with unpaid bills from clients. I had my first check in my hand and stood there for a moment when I realized that it had been years since I had physically received a paycheck. I opened it and stood in absolute amazement. The check was for twenty hours of training and after taxes the total amount came to $75.00. I was beside myself and stared at that piece of paper for a long time.

I said, 'God, thank you so much'.

In just a few years my income had shrunk from one containing many zeros to that simple payment of $75.00. It may sound silly, but I was so grateful that I shed a few heartfelt tears. It made me realize that my new home was a place that could give me the opportunity to take care of my family. I was truly blessed because I was getting paid to live and work in paradise.

That transition from one lifestyle to another was a lesson well learned so I believe it's important to illustrate here. Such major transitions in life will always teach a person what should be their priorities. For me, it proved that my family and my children were my ultimate treasures. I could only thank God for letting me discover those blessings. He must have heard me because the gifts continued to present themselves. One in particular came in the form of my nephew extending his hand to welcome my boys and me to live in his home. The feeling of family unity, love and support exuded from our new household over the next few months. Not only was the display of family bonding important to me, it was also priceless for my boys to be exposed to that type of positivity in a family structure.

Paradise: there is a reason why we label places with that special moniker. For some, paradise is a place of wealth and for others it's a place to escape from the complex world. For me, my paradise was a place that brought my boys and I closer to our family and where I felt safe.

The countless amenities in our town were invaluable. Above all else the school system was perhaps the most important. I was able to place my youngest son, Blake, into the area charter school. It was a great place for a child and the fact that they didn't have a busing system provided me the luxury of taking Blake to and from school every day. Each morning we would ride in the car and talk about what the day might bring; those times were so valuable. It allowed me time to tell him how much he meant to me and how proud he made me. In turn, he would share thoughts about his interests and aspirations in life. I miss those times more than ever and I realize just how lucky we were to be able to share such beautiful moments.

Dean, my middle son and six years Blake's senior, was also finding his way in paradise. He was such a unique and incredibly energetic person who was born with many amazing talents. However, as is common for most teenage boys, he encountered some struggles. I believe it was part in parcel because of the many times we had moved as a family. Those moves uprooted him in his life when it was critical to be able to establish solid long-term friendships. Over the course of our relationship we both have realized that I could have done a better job as a parent in some areas of his life.

While driving with Dean on a serene blue day, some feelings began to well up inside me. I had an overwhelming desire to discuss our relationship from the standpoint of mother and son. I decided to apologize for some of the decisions I made that had challenging effects on him. By apologizing I was delving deep into my soul to make amends. It was heart wrenching for both of us. The pain and forgiveness we shared during that car ride produced some of the most profound tears I've ever cried. From that day on our relationship began to evolve into something more concrete and meaningful.

By telling that story I want to magnify how extremely important it is for parents to express their shortcomings to their children; no matter how big or small they might be. On that drive with Dean I believe God intervened and helped me through the process in order to become a better mother and friend to my son.

As a mother, I had to learn to walk again as I was taken down a peg or two. While I worked so hard over the years to succeed in my career, I was unaware that I jeopardized the relationships I held with my children by doing so. I was unconsciously using the excuse of being my family's sole provider to justify my actions. Honestly, I admit that it was my decision to work hard throughout my career. As sure as I am sitting here, I believe it's truly the sole decision for someone to design their life from the inside. I'm fortunate that I stopped in my tracks so that I was able to see that paradise was the best place to be.

We all need that kind of support I received after making the decision to climb a mountain that I thought was absolutely insurmountable. A mountain that smacks you with menacing winds and a cold that is capable of freezing you solid in seconds. The difficult choice to climb, the choice to look life straight in the eye is one that made me stronger. It's a choice that would help me with one of the most treacherous things to happen to me in my life. All of my previous experiences to that point in my life would pale in comparison to what was about to come into my head.

All in My Head

Paradise was good to me in so many ways and after nearly three years as a design salesperson I decided to put my real-estate license to work. I spread my wings and moved into the sales division, selling homes. One beautiful spring morning I was out and about showing houses to prospective buyers. As I stood in the grand foyer of one of the homes giving an overview, an incredible searing pain shot through my left eye. It was so excruciating that I gasped for air.

"Are you alright Mary?" my customers asked me.

I answered, "I don't know. I'm in a lot of pain right now and I'm having trouble seeing."

We decided that it was best to take a break in order to let the pain sub-side; however, it became more intense. I couldn't bear it so we decided to head back to the office for another sales person to take over for me. After returning home I hoped to find some comfort by taking my migraine medication. To no avail, the pain continued and was so drastic that I soon found myself holding my head in my hands moaning in agony. Frantically, I picked up the phone and began calling friends and family for help. Finally— I was able to reach Angie, who was one of my close friends at the time and was able to come to my aid. After arriving at my house she found me in tears and grasping my head in desperation.

"What's wrong?" she asked.

I could only say, "I don't know. I'm in so much pain."

Wasting no time, she exclaimed, "Let's hurry and get you to the emergency room."

Bernadette met us at the hospital and she lovingly spent hours and most of the evening by my side as I dealt with an excruciating sickness. I was administered pain medication in the E.R. that helped me settle down before being taken in for a CAT scan. Surprisingly, the result of the scan was negative. I was relieved but couldn't understand how the CAT scan showed nothing wrong.

After keeping me for some time to make sure I was stable, the hospital decided that it was safe to release me.

When I woke the next morning I felt strong enough to take on a day of work (yes, I went into work). I was tired but also thankful that the pain had subsided enough for me to get through the day. I called my sister Bernadette to let her know I was all right. She told me that she talked to my brother Denny and he suggested I get a magnetic resonance angiogram (MRA). An MRA is a type of MRI that uses a magnetic field and pulses of radio wave energy to capture images of blood vessels inside the body. The scan is capable of providing more information than other tests such as x-rays and ultrasounds (it's an MRI on steroids if you will). My sister told me that by having the scan done it could possibly find out what was causing my severe headaches.

As I usually do, I took my sister's wise advice and contacted the hospital to set up an appointment. Surprisingly, the scan only took a couple of hours and afterwards I was able to leave the hospital with a positive reassuring skip in my step. After a day of work, later that evening I went home and was greeted by the blinking red light that beamed from my answering machine. I hit play.

"Hello Ms. Cook. This is the radiology center calling. We need you to contact us as soon as possible," the hospital had said.

I wasn't able to call back just then so I let it slide for the night and planned to call first thing in the morning. Before I had the chance to call back the hospital was calling me again.

The voice on the other side of the line said, "Hi Ms. Cook. We need to know where you are."

I said, "I'm at work. Why?"

They said, "Well, we need you to stop what you're doing and have someone drive you to the hospital immediately."

"Why?" I asked

"Well, you have a brain aneurysm," they said.

"What?!" I was flabbergasted.

When someone breaks that type of powerful news to you, I can assure you, it feels like a dream.

"I'm sorry to inform you but you've been diagnosed with having a brain aneurysm. You must proceed to the hospital immediately for additional tests. Your condition is extremely dangerous. We've learned that the aneurysm is located in a specific area of your lower brain that is particularly alarming. It's absolutely critical that we get you here as soon as possible. I'm also instructed to tell you that a second aneurysm, albeit smaller aneurysm, was also detected."

I was stunned. I couldn't breathe or make sense of anything; it had to be a nightmare. Just five minutes before I figured I was in the clear and that the MRA would be the ultimate test to prove it. The severity of the situation began to sink in and I realized that my life was in jeopardy. I remember repeating to myself, "Why is this happening?"

My brother Denny and I immediately went to the hospital's pre-op center to register. When I first talked to the doctors they let me know that I had to have an angiogram. An angiogram is a procedure that is necessary to verify the results of an MRA. They scheduled it for the next morning, checked my vital signs and then relinquished me back into my brother's care for the night. As Denny and I left the hospital we started thinking of how we were going to break the distressing news to my family. We certainly knew that difficult times were on the horizon.

At the time my parents were living with my sister, Bernadette. Denny and I decided it would be best to let them know first so they wouldn't be caught off guard if they heard the news from somewhere else. We entered Bernadette's house and she instantly knew something was wrong.

"What is going on?" my sister asked.

My brother took her by the hand and as they sat, Denny explained my situation and a sullen look came over my sister's face. I could see that she was beside herself – her eyes began to fill with tears. Bernadette and her husband are strong individuals who have always inspired me. Perhaps their most endearing trait is how much they enjoy acting as caregivers; so after hearing of my condition, her heart immediately went out to me. She quickly re-gained her composure and expressed that it would be best to bring our parents over so we could inform them of the life threatening situation we were all now a part of. At that moment, as we sat in their living room, I became overwhelmed by the strength and love that was radiating from my brother and sister. They knew it would be difficult for me to be brave, so they forcefully displayed a beautiful courage for me. I lovingly thanked them and realized all I could do was take their lead.

When my parents came into the room I didn't hesitate, I plainly told them that I was diagnosed with a brain aneurysm and that I would be going through tests over the next few days. They were shocked and stunned for a few moments; almost in denial. My mom began to cry and my dad repeatedly insisted that the tests were wrong. I couldn't hold my tears back any longer so I began to sob as well.

I thought to myself, "How have I made it this far in life only to learn that I might only have a short time left?"

Breaking the news to my parents was difficult but I was assured they had the strength and faith to handle the situation. However, I was worried about how my sons would react to the news. My boys weren't accustomed to dealing with such life threatening situations, in particular, my son Blake. For years I was practically Blake's only sense of parental guidance so I knew I had to deliver the news with great care. I felt the best thing to do was to tell my boys individually. When Blake returned from school that day, I looked to God for the strength to tell him without sending danger signals. I took his hand and sat with him on the sofa and began to explain. The wave of horror that moved across his face instantly ripped me apart. I hope no parent is ever faced with that type of emotional distress. After putting Blake at ease the best I knew how… we made it through that very tough talk. I then felt ready to let my older boys know about my medical condition.

So there it was, all laid out for my family to digest and process. That evening my sister graciously spent the night comforting me and refused to leave my side. I can never repay Bernadette for her sacrifice and love: what an angel.

The next morning we headed off to the hospital. As we drove out of the garage, I remember turning the radio on and instantly it was like God was reaching out to me. There, as we sat stunned listening to Josh Groban singing his song 'You Raise Me Up', it was so inspirational and the timing couldn't have been better. We both felt like we could endure anything. Once at the hospital, I was bombarded by a myriad of people whose job it was to prepare me for the angiogram. If you don't know what an angiogram is, here is a quick description:

Angiography or *Arteriography*: *a medical imaging technique used to visualize the inside, or lumen, of blood vessels and organs of the body, with particular interest in the arteries and veins. This is traditionally done by injecting a radio-opaque contrast agent into the blood vessel and imaging using x-ray based techniques such as fluoroscopy.*

I learned that during an angiograph the patient is not sedated and that it's critical that they be completely immobilized. To do so, a thick wide leather strap was brought across my chin to set my head into position. Once I was immobilized the doctors could begin the test. Throughout the process I had to answer the doctor's sporadic questions to assure them I was conscious. Steel wires were injected through my femoral artery (groin), up through my arterial system and then finally into my brain. The wires (sheathes) were used to inject my aneurysm with a radio-opaque contrast agent. Once the agent was spread throughout the aneurysm, a fluoroscopy (x-ray) would be used to reveal the best way to treat the malformation. After approximately two hours, the doctors were able to thoroughly examine the aneurysm.

After the test I was groggy from the pain medication and from not eating beforehand. Naturally, I began to vomit. Through a sickly fog I could barely make out the doctor as he entered my room. I can remember Bernadette having a pensive expression on her face because she knew the doctor was about to give us the test results.

"I have some good news and I have some challenging news. Which news do you want first?" he asked.

I certainly wasn't ready for any bad news at the moment so I looked up at him and said, "The good news. Please, only the good news."

"Well, the aneurysm is not at the base of your brain as we had first thought," the doctor told me.

"O.K., great," I said

As his demeanor and tone changed, he let me know that I was about to hear the bad news.

He explained, "Unfortunately the aneurysm is located behind your left eye in the carotid and ophthalmic artery. It's an open ended aneurysm and it's in a position that we feel may make it impossible to operate on."

"So what does that mean?" I asked.

He answered, "It means that we feel there might not be a solution. It's probable that the aneurysm will rupture at some point."

I can remember how sick I felt and how the news brought the hammer down upon my world. It was impossible for me to process the finality of the doctor's statement, but it was there in all of its simplicity. I remember looking at my sister and feeling so lost and so alone that I would never be found. Hopelessness washed over my soul. My nausea escalated to such an excruciating level that the doctor decided to keep me on close watch through the night. I spent hours writhing in pain with an indescribable sickness. Finally, I calmed down when some pain medication took hold of my body. At last, I was able to sleep.

The next morning my doctor let me know that he researched my condition through the night. He believed the best course of action was to refer me to a facility in Gainesville, FL. The facility, he had learned, had the potential to handle a case as severe as mine. Although I felt exhausted both mentally and physically, the prospect of such good medical treatment gave me a glimmer of hope. Once again, the doctor checked my vital signs and gave me clearance to return to the comfort of my own home to regain my strength. Once home, I called the hospital in Gainesville hoping to learn whether or not they might have the missing piece to my body's puzzle.

In the meantime, the next day, I went back to work and was quickly reminded that it's impossible to place a value on great co-workers. That first day back my boss unexpectedly called me to her office. She had some information that she thought I might be interested in.

She asked, "Well first off, how are you feeling?"

"I'm feeling alright but I'm worried about what's going to happen next. I'm not sure what to do about a lot of things," I said.

She responded, "I'm glad you're feeling better. Listen, I have some information you might like to hear. I have a couple of recommendations for your future treatment, that is, if you're open to the idea."

"Heck yes I am! Are you kidding?" I yelled.

She let me know that she might be able to get me in touch with one of the leading healthcare clinics in the nation that was located in Jacksonville, FL. My eyes lit up with a spark of hope. With so much worry and stress surrounding me, the wind had been taken from my sails – that little piece of information was enough to set my internal jib high and lifted me up. I was unquestionably grateful to my boss for taking the time to extend her hand to me.

With her and her family's help, they contacted the hospital in Jacksonville and a consultation was set up along with a full day of tests (I was becoming a semi-professional tester). As Denny and I headed to the hospital for that big day a profound and courageous feeling of hope began to rise within me.

The tests came and went all day. I felt like I was caught up in whirling tornado of medical procedures. After my tests subsided I met another very kind physician who was a slender man who exuded great confidence.

He kindly said, "After reviewing your MRA scans, we've learned how unique and challenging your situation is going to be. But please don't fret. I believe I have a doctor on staff who can tackle the problem."

The doctor continued, "From the scans, we know how difficult it's going to be to reach the aneurysm due to the location. That area of your brain is incredibly delicate; it's an area that's very dangerous to tamper with. The doctor whom I'm going to recommend may be one of the best in his field. I feel that if there's a chance anyone can help, it's him. Can I possibly get you to stay in town overnight so that you two can meet tomorrow?"

My brother and I yelled out, "Are you crazy? We'll stay a week if we need to."

To our surprise the doctor grabbed a phone right then to make a call. When it connected, I could hear a friendly and chipper voice on the other end ring out.

"Hello! This is Dr. Miller's nurse, Mary. How can I help you?" she said (it was way cool, her name was Mary too).

My doctor said, "I have a patient in front of me that I think Dr. Miller should see. He might be one of the few physicians who have the skills to help."

I was instantly blown away by the nurse's friendly and kind spirit; she quickly found a way into my heart. Her attitude and determination just in finding me some time in her doctor's demanding schedule struck a chord. Not only was she exactly the type of person I needed help from, it was also clear how confident and trusting she was in the doctor's expertise. The man I'm speaking about is

Dr. Miller: a brilliant and gifted interventional neuro-radiologist. When Mary let me know Dr. Miller could take my case my heart nearly leapt from my chest. The dynamic combo of Nurse Mary and Dr. Miller would be the radiating force to carry me through that life-threatening situation.

I will never forget when Mary called. It felt like I was talking to an angel who was helping to save my life. I can only thank her from the depths of my soul and let her know how much it meant. Mary and I had an immediate connection, one beyond the fact that our names are the same. During our initial conversation she asked me several important questions and informed me that Dr. Miller was already aware of my condition. We set an appointment but unfortunately Mary wasn't able to attend. Although she didn't need to be there for the meeting, she went out of her way to apologize for her absence and to wish me the best of luck. This is what is so endearing about her. I believe that small loving gestures like those are sent directly from God. I truly felt Mary was an angel sent to me from the heavens.

After I hung up the phone I knew immediately the grand blessing that had been bestowed upon me. That night my brother and I celebrated with a nice dinner. We both felt as though we were in the middle of a divine intervention.

The following day Denny and I arrived for the big consultation. As we waited I thought about how special it was to be treated by such a well renowned physician; therefore, I was ready to wait as long as it took. Two and a half hours passed and we finally found ourselves walking down a corridor to meet my new doctor. The hall was aglow with cold neon lights and daunting sounds. As I approach his office suddenly I began to have a small panic attack – my nerves were getting the best of me. Instantly, I was put at ease by the warmth and inviting presence of the hospital's staff.

As I entered Dr. Miller's office, the fact that this doctor just might save my life hit me hard. To my brother's and my surprise the office wasn't one you would think a highly respected doctor would have. It was a smaller room, a bit confining at about only 10' x 10' foot. The room could only fit a small round table and three chairs. Dr. Miller's walls were covered with books about nuclear medicine and other neurological procedures. Nuclear medicine intrigued Denny because he had been commissioned on a nuclear submarine in the Navy.

After some time of observing the talented doctor's domain, the office door burst open and in walked the handsome Dr. Miller. He was clad in his O.R. scrubs and greeted us with a heartwarming smile.

"Well, there you are Mary," Dr. Miller said.

After extending his hand I playfully said, "Wow! Here I am!"

He proceeded to sit down in front of Denny and I to present us with my x-rays.

He re-assured me by saying, "Mary, I think we may be able to help you."

My eyes immediately swelled and ballooned with tears as I quietly said my thanks to God. He wanted to shed some light on the situation so he started describing the difficulty of the surgery.

"Mary, on a scale of one to ten your aneurysm is about 9½," he said.

The statement was brief and I could tell that he just wanted to make a point. Although he spoke in medial terms Dr. Miller did a wonderful job in helping me to understand what was happening.

As he spoke my brother and I listened intently.

He continued, "There are two treatment options commonly used for aneurysms. One customary method of dealing with aneurysms is to drill down thorough the skull with a specialized saw: this procedure is called a craniotomy. Unfortunately, because your aneurysm is so intricately placed a craniotomy isn't possible. The second treatment option that we will use is called an *endovascular coiling* – but with a twist.

The Anatomy of an Operation

Dr. Miller continued, "It is common for most aneurysms to be shaped like a balloon with a narrow entrance. However, your aneurysm is unique in that it's open ended, meaning that it has a wide entrance. That wide end of the aneurysm is why we need to be creative in how we proceed. We will insert two catheters into your body. The first will pass through the femoral artery located in the groin, then through your carotid artery, up into your brain arteries and then finally into the aneurysm itself. Then we will be able to inject platinum coils that will close the aneurysm off to prevent it from rupturing."

Calmly, he continued, "The second catheter will be fed through the same system, but its sole purpose is to use a microscopic balloon to hold the coils in place so they can't escape into your arterial system. That would be catastrophic."

I was frozen dead in my tracks. Hearing the intricate details of what would actually be taking place certainly seemed like a bone chilling procedure. Dr. Miller continued, "The coils are critical – they initiate a clotting or thrombotic reaction that, if successful, will secure the aneurysm."

I had heard of similar, scary explanations regarding medical procedures; but when I realized I was directly involved a wave of fear pulsed through me. From my perspective, it all seemed like science fiction.

The next order of business for me was to pass a number of neurological exams. Dr. Miller began asking various questions about my health and immediately I remembered a sense of camaraderie swelling in the air. Dr. Miller, Denny and I knew how important it was to stay positive and to keep things light so we made sure to crack a joke or two. Somehow we found a way to laugh and set each other at ease. There was an obvious bond developing between Dr. Miller and me. As we became closer I began to feel very comfortable around him. Comfort is one thing; faith is another. There was just one thing I had to know before I put my life into his hands.

I looked Dr. Miller directly in the eyes and asked, "Do you believe in God?"

He said, "Mary, I couldn't do what I do each and every day without knowing that God is using me as a vehicle to help people."

That was all I needed to hear. It was then and only then that I felt at ease with my choice to move ahead. The exam came to an end when we heard a knock at the door; in peered a lovely lady with a beautiful smile.

She said, "Well, I did make it in time."

There she was, Mary, the angel that spoke to me on the phone and who was instrumental in helping me along the winding path I was on. It dawned on me that she decided to come to the hospital even though she had a previous family commitment. Denny and I both leapt to our feet and greeted her with a grizzly bear hug. After talking for about an hour I was amazed at how fast of friends we had all become. Dr. Miller and Mary must have dealt with hundreds of patients a year and yet somehow, they found time to make me feel as if I was the only patient on their schedule. It's impossible to put the importance of that meeting into words; all I can say is that it changed the course of my life. They even took the time to walk Denny and I out of the hospital! That type of doctor/patient treatment is something that is very uncommon in today's healthcare industry.

After driving back to paradise, Denny and I decided to stop at Bernadette's house so we could let everyone know about the incredible news. When I told my mom, dad and Bernadette that I had learned that there was a solution to my illness, with eyes full of tears, they all gave me warm embraces. A sense of relief had washed over us for the time being.

I was lucky to have been placed in the path of Mary and Dr. Miller so I quickly felt that my life was being taken into celestial hands. I believe that my faith in God is what would ultimately carry me through that most difficult time. The next day Mary informed me that the procedure was scheduled for the following week and she let me know what to expect: the date was set in stone and there was no stopping us from conquering the challenge.

Fine – but I can say that it wasn't going to be easy!

Virgin Territory

If you've never had major surgery before then I can only do my best to describe the feeling and emotions that take place before the big day arrives. A few days before the surgery my anxiety levels were off the charts, I was visibly shaken. It was difficult to steady my hands so I did my best to not only ease my fears but the fears of my family. I focused on keeping my mind occupied so I decided to drive to the hospital in hopes of keeping my focus. Bernadette and I decided to head to Jacksonville a few days before the surgery so that we could enjoy some R & R at the hotel. Once again, my sister Bernadette was there to support me in any way that she could. Denny decided it best to stay home so that he could look after my mom and dad. I knew that Bernadette was an amazing caregiver so I felt comfortable in the fact that I would be well taken care of.

On the morning of the big day we woke early and headed for the hospital. After waiting some time Dr. Miller arrived with his usual jovial appearance. However, I could tell something was amiss because I instantly noticed that Mary wasn't by his side.

Dr. Miller said, "Today is Mary's birthday. Her husband surprised her by whisking her off to California. She wanted you to know that she's sorry for not being here for you. There will be a short wait and then we'll take you to get prepped for surgery. Then we'll truly be on our way to taking care of this once and for all."

Dr. Miller knew how confident I was in his capabilities as a surgeon. He also recognized that Mary's presence, throughout all of it, was very important to me. The doctor knew that as well because she was an irreplaceable part of the plan. Realizing that I missed Mary, Dr. Miller thoughtfully tried to keep the atmosphere as light and positive as possible. After taking some time to settle me down, he was off and back to his normal routine.

Some time passed and we were beginning to feel antsy when one of the floor nurses came in and said, "Hello ladies. I need to let you know that Dr. Miller was pulled into an emergency surgery. He's in the operating room. Once he has completed the surgery you are next on our schedule." My sister and I certainly didn't anticipate this bump in the road but we understood these things happen, especially in the hospital environment. That's the way life is. At the time all I could do was pray for the patient Dr. Miller was attending to; that person's condition certainly seemed critical. It is safe to say that in hospitals there can never be enough hope or prayers being spread to those who need it most.

As Bernadette and I prayed, something began to sidetrack me: it was the rumbling in my stomach! I hadn't had a bite to eat or practically anything to drink for at least a day. As the hours passed by it became more difficult to push on. Minutes turned into hours and still no word of when my surgery might begin. Eleven hours passed and I was ready to smash the glass casing of a nearby vending machine. That's when Bernadette and I were approached by a new doctor; he informed us that Dr. Miller was just finishing the emergency procedure and would be out to speak with me in a moment. A few minutes later an extremely exhausted Dr. Miller approached us while still wearing his O.R. scrubs. He sat down in front of us with his head bent low and with a somber look on his face; he began to explain the situation.

"Mary, an emergency situation occurred. It was life threatening so I needed to perform surgery immediately to keep the patient alive," he explained.

The surgery was extremely taxing and had exhausted not only him, but his entire team. Regretfully, he explained that the time wasn't right to proceed with my surgery. I was deeply disappointed but I understood completely.

My sister and I were frozen in time. I could hardly breathe when I realized I would have to start the pre-op process from scratch. I was happy for the person that Dr. Miller helped, but I couldn't help feel somewhat dejected. It's an arduous task to explain how much emotional energy and strength it takes to prepare for such an operation; both the mental and physical dedication is beyond draining. I thought I would just fall to pieces.

It was the reassurance of Dr. Miller and my sister that lifted my spirits. He is truly one of the kindest and most compassionate people I've encountered on this earth. I knew in my heart that if he felt there was a possibility to move ahead, he would have chosen to do so. He told us that there was no way the surgery could take place within less than a week. His team needed time to regroup in order to be prepared for the level of surgery that was required. As my sister and I prepared to leave the hospital, Dr. Miller went that extra step by offering us his direct contact number.

He said, "Please, if there's anything you need or have worries about don't hesitate for a moment to use that number."

Dr. Miller will never know how much that meant to me in one of my great times of need. But trouble was on the horizon. Heading back to the hotel with my sister I became nauseous and violently ill. Figuring it was just a side effect from not eating, I dismissed the feeling as a passing ailment. However, I soon began to heave my guts out and found myself lying on the bathroom floor writhing in agony. The nausea and vomiting I could handle, however, I believe it was the severe emotional stress that was beginning to cause the stinging headaches.

My major concern wasn't my upset stomach it was the intense pressure in my head that started to mount. The pain finally reached its apex and I could no longer withstand it. Bernadette contacted Dr. Miller immediately to fill him in and I could see the panic in my sister's eyes. Her demeanor frightened me more than anything else. I knew Bernadette had cared for many sick people in her life and had been involved in numerous life threatening situations; so seeing the worry in her eyes set me aback. Hence, I feared for the worst.

Dr. Miller urged us not to hesitate for a moment and that it was detrimental that I return to the emergency room: STAT! I was so ill that I could barely walk to the car. I had to use all of my strength (as well as my sister's) to make our way back to the hospital. The attending physician in the E.R. gave me an injection that was meant to ease my nausea. The sickness was so overwhelming that just one injection wasn't strong enough to curb the vomiting. I was given a second stab and finally the sickness began to fade.

When Dr. Miller was freed of his responsibilities he made his way into my room. The attending physician and my sister tried their best to catch him up as to my condition.

"Well doctor, she's been violently ill so I administered anti-nausea medication. Now it seems as though she's hallucinating just a bit," said the attending physician.

I vaguely remember saying to my sister, "Hey Bernadette, you look like that dog in the picture hanging on the wall, you're fluffy! And when did you get that big bushy tail, it's so pretty! Oh, hello Dr. Miller. Um, why are you dressed like that? Are you going fishing today? Hospitals aren't a good place to find fish."

Due to the fact that I hadn't eaten while combining powerful medication at the same time, I was certain that Elvis passed by my room (thank you very much). The whole night was quite the adventure. When Dr. Miller checked on me the next morning, thankfully, the hallucinations had subsided, as had my nausea. I let him know that I was feeling better but exhausted. The good doctor was relieved to learn that the night's ordeal had rendered itself quiet.

"That's great Mary, glad to have you back. And to let you know, just for you, I've canceled my daily fishing trip to the O.R.," he always knew how to calm me down with witty lighthearted jokes.

He softly put his hand on my arm to say, "Mary, you are going to be just fine. However, I need you to head home in order to regain your strength once again. You must understand that we're hoping to schedule your surgery in the coming week. Your strength is vital to its success."

The confidence that emanated from Dr. Miller's eyes leveled me. I felt strong in trusting him with my life and I knew without a doubt, that he was the perfect person for my unique situation. I was also ecstatic to learn that Mary would be returning just in time to be with me for my surgery. Dr. Miller knew how close the two of us 'Mary's' had become. The news calmed me down so much that I fell into a restful slumber.

The next day I had to return home to let everyone know the surgery wouldn't be for at least a few more days. This ultimately meant more time spent worrying about and fearing the unknown. Not only was I drained, but I felt terrible for having to put my family through so much emotional stress. I needed to let them know the worst was not over and their unconditional support was the most important thing to me.

My family expressed their love and reassured me they were the concrete foundation that I could rest upon no matter what obstacle arose. After a bit of coaxing, we all felt it best that I return to work to distract my mind and reinstate some normalcy into my life: little did I know what lay ahead. I walked into the office and was greeted by an immense out-pouring of love and support. Unbeknownst to me, in my absence, many caring but also confused emails had been circulating throughout the office. My associates were only informed about my condition through the preverbal grapevine. From the good of their hearts, they wanted to show their support when I returned. What great love! It was as if my co-works had become a second family and were all there to support me completely. I believe God was behind it all.

On-Q

In the following days, right on queue, I received the heavily anticipated phone call from my favorite nurse, Mary. She was back from California and it was time to get into the specifics of when my surgery would be scheduled. After one of our infamous girl-to-girl "pow-wows", she snapped me back to reality.

"Mary, this next week will be critical for you. This is real. It's going to happen and it is going to be a success," she said with such vigor.

To say I was floating on cloud nine after pressing the end button would be a gross understatement. The surgery was now solidified; we would attack the aneurysm and eliminate it once and for all.

Bernadette continued her saintly ways and proposed that we take a few days before the surgery to relax and spend time together. We secured a hotel room with a cozy pool that would pander to our needs. My sister and I were slowly beginning to feel the immediacy of the surgery's impending timeframe; therefore, we wanted to enjoy quality time. My brother Denny had returned to Michigan after the surgery's first delay; however, the nut called to inform us he was jumping into his car and driving back to Jacksonville through the night just to be by my side. To say the least, my spirit rose immensely.

It was Memorial Day weekend. The Florida heat and humidity was earning its name as some the nation's most punishing conditions. As Bernadette and I started out for the hotel not only did the stifling heat strike me like a hot bullet, but I realized the congested Memorial Day traffic might impede Denny's arrival. It was Sunday morning and my surgery was scheduled for early Tuesday; the three of us desperately wanted that Monday together to spend as a family. As fortune would have it, Denny beat the traffic that allowed us enough time to collect our thoughts. There we were: three pillars standing strong and ready for the challenging surgery.

On the morning of the surgery, I focused on trying to prepare myself for what lay ahead. The only problem was; I had no idea what to expect. After arriving at the hospital and being admitted, the attending anesthesiologist spent time reviewing what his role would be throughout my hospital stay. I was certain to let him know of my prior battles with nausea.

"I just want to let you know that I experienced terrible side effects from the anti-nausea medication that I was administered last time. And by side effects I mean hallucinations and puking my lungs up!" I said in jovial way to keep the mood light.

After getting my point across, he reassured me that I would have no problem handling the anesthesia. In walked Dr. Miller and Mary, just their presence calmed me. They greeted me kindly and took a moment to set my heart at ease. Then they proceeded to inform me of what to expect.

Hope floated throughout my spirit. Just seeing Mary calmed my nerves. Her voice and smile could paint any room with sunshine; she had a spell on me that was hard to explain. With my loved ones surrounding me and with God in my soul I felt ready for the surgery. I was at peace with the world and gave myself over to God. They wheeled me into the O.R. and Dr. Miller touched my hand.

I was then administered the anesthesia and quickly fell into a calm slumber.

My eyes slowly began to open. The room was a-blur with florescent glows and hypnotic pulsating beeps. As my vision began to sharpen things began to register. The most important and special people at that time in my life came into focus: Dr. Miller and Mary. They were leaning over the bed so as to assure me I wasn't alone. Seeing their warm smiles comforted me. I wasn't sick from the anesthesia so I believed that everything had gone smoothly — not so fast!

As I came back to consciousness and began to speak, I was overcome by great fatigue. Dr. Miller assured me it was all right to go back to sleep so that's exactly what I did. It was during that sleep that I had a vivid dream: in my dream Mary approached me.

She said, "Now, I don't want you to worry. We weren't able to secure the aneurysm but we will get it fixed the next time around."

I awoke shortly thereafter and found Bernadette on one side of me while Denny was on the other. After getting my bearings yet again, I was about to explain the dream to them when Dr. Miller and Mary entered the room. I remember it as though it was yesterday.

Dr. Miller looked directly into my eyes and said, "Look Mary, I was unable to finish the procedure because my equipment was not operating at the level that it needed to. Due to the difficult placement of the aneurysm and how delicate this all is, the equipment wasn't proving to be reliable enough."

I was stunned.

I could only think, "Am I really hearing this correctly? The equipment failed?"

The only thing I could think to ask was, "So, when will I be fixed?"

He responded immediately, "I have spoken to the equipment's manufacturer. They're sending a technician as soon as possible to get this situation resolved."

"O.K., how long will it take?" I asked.

Dr. Miller replied, "Well, they're going to run diagnostics on the equipment and then let me know when I can expect to use it again."

I couldn't find any words and remember looking to Mary for an answer as if she supposed to have one. I stared at her momentarily like she was about to pull a rabbit out of a hat.

Dr. Miller took a deep breath. He then said, "Mary, I'm going to recommend that you go to our main hospital in Minnesota. Two of my colleagues, who I have previously trained with and whom I hold in the highest regard will be able to complete the procedure. They work closely together and have developed a tandem system. If one of the performing surgeons is unable to execute the procedure, the other is there for backup. In all it's a two-man system with perhaps the most sophisticated technology. Hence, we feel this is the best answer to our challenge."

I was bewildered. I couldn't believe what I was hearing. I can vividly remember feeling like I was living a horrific dream; unfortunately, I was surrounded by a harsh reality. They stood there like hallow statues in wait of my response. I wanted to hide and escape by sprouting wings that would let me fly away from all of my troubles.

I took a deep bellowing breath and burst out, "No!"

Everyone in the room fell silent with only light gasps from my brother and sister filling the air. A rush of euphoria swept my body out to sea. I believed that somehow it was God's will and that the surgery's outcome, no matter what, was my destiny alone. If God's plan was that I wasn't meant to survive my surgery, then accepting his will was my only option.

I surprised myself. I had no fight left in my soul and I knew it. Although I felt weak and defeated, I began to feel an inner peace rising up within me. The doctors had done everything possible to keep me on this earth but it was apparent that it probably wasn't going to be enough.

It's difficult to describe what I saw in front me, there were two lovely people standing there who were not a part of my family. They weren't lifelong friends with whom I'd shared countless experiences with; they were simply people who cared and loved me as if I was one of their own. I wanted Mary and Dr. Miller to know how deeply I appreciated them and what they were doing. It seemed to me that they felt they were losing one of their closest family members.

Dr. Miller sat next to me and bravely said, "Mary, I would go to Minnesota if I needed this procedure. It's where I would send my sister if she needed it. These doctors are the best. I know because I've trained with them. I know you've heard that statement before but I have complete confidence in sending you there. Please, find the strength to go."

I took his words to heart but I was still content to let God carry out his plans. Once again, I gave praise to them both and let them know that I would be heading home the following day. It was Dr. Miller's goal to keep me in the hospital as long as possible so he was using the technician as a pawn. He wanted to wait for the equipment to be checked before I left to ensure that the surgery wasn't possible. As Dr. Miller and Mary left my room, I noticed Mary glance over her shoulder at me with a look that told me she understood why I was making the decision not to go to Minnesota. She understood me completely and knew that I needed more time to think about the situation. The truth was that I was facing the possibility of dying. I needed time to be with my family so to help them understand my decision.

It was morning and my exhausted mind awoke to the world. The skies were shaded with tones of gray and heavy rains pelted angrily against my hospital room window. The somber weather wasn't what I was hoping for. I hoped for baby blue hues and sunshine to lighten my spirits. It was one of the first times I could feel God's earthly affect playing on my mood. My life was now amplified and nature took on a new face. I looked out into the gusts of drab winds and felt a downward slide seeping into my heart.

I prayed, "If only the sun would peek through the clouds it would help me along."

Realizing that every moment on earth was becoming more and more precious, I remember wanting to encompass everything life had to offer. I didn't want a somber atmosphere to bring me down so I tried my best to put on a brave face.

Dr. Miller and Mary entered my hospital room once again and started, "I'm sorry to say it's going to take a significant amount of time to repair the equipment necessary for your surgery. Mary, I'm sticking to my guns and recommending that you head off to Minnesota to see the surgeons there."

All I could say was, "Thank you both from the bottom of my heart for all of your dedication and love. But I think it's time to go home. I've made my decision. It's final." Dr. Miller's eyes were sullen and said that he and Mary respected my decision but would call to check on me in a few days.

The ride home to paradise was a trip to remember. My brother decided that he wanted to spend as much time with me as he could so he followed us back home. Bernadette and I didn't speak much because of the somber and disparaging mood. My thoughts swirled as the rain constantly pelted our car. There was a mixture of fear as well as confusion.

I thought, "Why is this happening?"

After dropping Bernadette and Denny off so that I could be alone, I drove home. As I pulled into the garage I can remember feeling the most exhausted I had been since my medical journey began. It was as though the bubble in my brain had totally sucked every emotion I ever had in my life right out of my body. All I wanted to do was get home to my wonderful cocoon, drop my suitcase down and curl up in my soft warm bed. I must be honest; I was giving up. The decision to let go of life was weighing down on me like a menacing concrete blanket. Giving up went against everything in my character; I never gave up on anything. However, I had never been faced with a challenge like this.

When I walked into the kitchen I sat my keys down on the counter, went to the refrigerator and grabbed a bottle of water before going to lie down. I reached in for the water and turned to walk to my bedroom. It was exactly what I needed before heading off to bed.

Suddenly there it was – the beautiful picture of my mother and father. Immediate, transcendent warmth washed over me and absorbed my world with peace.

Before lying down I sat on the edge of my bed, looked to the heavens and said, "I am sorry, God, for making this decision. But I just can't go on like this anymore. I hope you will understand my choice and that you will help my family and I deal with whatever comes next."

As I slid under my satin covers the exhaustion transformed into a magnificent feeling of gratefulness. I folded my hands together and said a small prayer, thanking God for my blessed life. At the end of my prayer I threw God a kiss and then slowly closed my eyes and drifted off into a soft peaceful slumber.

After a day of rest and hiding out from the world, I decided to try and figure out how I really wanted to live my life. At the same time I began to plan for what I thought was the inevitable. On my third day of hiding the phone rang and on the other end I heard Dr. Miller's warm voice with Mary by his side.

"How are you feeling?" his voice echoed out.

I told him that I was feeling fine and he followed with the most direct question he ever asked me.

"When can we start making plans for you to go north to get this taken care of?" the kind doctor asked bluntly.

I was beside myself. It had been three days since I spoke with Dr. Miller, I had settled into a comfort zone by hiding out for a while. During those quiet days I came to peace with what my ultimate destiny might be and chose to dedicate myself to loving every remaining minute of my life. That phone call from the Dr. Miller certainly rang my 'bell' and my response to his question shocked even me. There was no control in my answer, I wanted to say no but I blurted out: YES, I'M READY!

I said, "O.K. I'm ready, let's do it!"

I continued to ask Dr. Miller, "Did I really just say that?"

"You most certainly did Mary. Great, you don't know how happy this makes us all. My staff and I will contact you in the next few days and inform you of the plans to go to Minnesota."

The medical chess game was back on and my fear quickly had me wanting to morph into Bobby Fischer. I wanted to put my pieces in place for battle so I started alerting family members of the impending charge. The board had to be aligned so that everything would fall into place. After so much intense apprehension and spiritual exploration, it was time for me to push forward. Finally, after waiting, I received the call that would set the game in motion. Mary informed me that the surgery would take place in approximately one week. One week, seven days, that was it.

I understood that my aneurysm was in a tricky location, directly behind my left eye in the ophthalmic and carotid artery. I was also aware of the risk factors during the course of the procedure. One of the risk factors was that I could lose my sight; possibly waking up blind.

At that time, I decided nothing was going to get me down or dampen my spirits. I prepared for one of the scenarios; so I began to think like a blind person. You read that correctly. I knew it was critical that I learned how to get around as someone who couldn't see. Therefore, I began training myself how to navigate through my house with my eyes closed. Hours were spent maneuvering and exploring my living space without me having the luxury of sight (and I ultimately bumped into every nook and cranny). I believed that if prepared, I would be able to embrace my destiny no matter what the outcome.

Angel's Wings

Ironically, it was my birthday when I took flight for Minnesota: oh, what a birthday. Denny, bless his heart, drove from Florida back to Michigan. Then, he drove to greet my sister and me at the airport in Minnesota – that little engine could and he certainly did. Denny then drove us two hours through torrential rains again to reach the hospital.

Three grueling days were necessary for testing that would assure I was ready for surgery. I was able to share quality time with the hospital staff that would be performing the operation. The anesthesiologist assured me that I wouldn't get sick from the anesthesia. After reviewing the new head scans with the surgeons we learned of disheartening news. Doctors informed us that the aneurysm had grown nearly three times its original size. Not only had the primary aneurysm grown but a second aneurysm had developed outside the original one as well. This is called a mother-daughter aneurysm. We all knew that it was a race against time.

The negatives continued to pile up and were ultimately beating up on the positives; however, my spirit was about to receive a huge lift. That weekend I got a surprise visit from one of my dearest friends who was a former colleague. When he heard of my situation he decided to make the trip to Minnesota with his wife just to spend the weekend before my surgery. It's been said a million times before and I have no problem with saying it one more time: friends are priceless. Seeing them and knowing that I was in their prayers filled me with a newfound energy. I cannot place a value on what their demonstration of friendship meant to me.

They understood the severity of my situation so they made it a point to try and distract me. The weekend was filled with some necessary pre-surgery partying! We all enjoyed intimate dinners, drank wine and just took some time to laugh. It was an incredible weekend and a gift that I could never return.

As they departed I tried to rest their hearts by telling them everything would work out fine and I'd see them soon. They had surrounded me with so much love that I wanted to send them off with nothing but the same. The next morning Denny, Bernadette and I headed to the hospital. The new facility was certainly different than the other quaint hospitals I had been in before – it was the mother ship of healthcare facilities. To put into context it is a hospital that has seen its share of high profile clientele. The hospital was enormous; it instantly made me feel like a tiny person who was about to board a shuttle to the moon. I was admitted and quickly thereafter began to feel the painful absence of Dr. Miller and Mary. They had been such strong stones in my foundation throughout the ordeal and now I was without them. Things were moving quickly and each passing minute was a step closer to the surgery time. I found the strength to suppress my need for Dr. Miller and Mary to be by my side. I chose to feel confident in placing my destiny in the skilled hands of whoever was able to do the job.

Finally, the definitive time had come. I was wheeled into the operating room with a pounding heart and a determined spirit. The surgeons tried their best to put me at ease with customary reassuring banter. As the needle slid into my vein, I knew this was it. I believed I would wake up to the world I loved and be rid of my illness. The sedative began to set in and I began to sail out.

Spinning room. Muttered voices. Confusion. Arctic temperatures. These are the only things I can remember when I woke up several hours later. The voices I vaguely heard were those of the nurses asking me questions.

They all said, "Come on Mary, wake up! Let's talk."

I tried but I just couldn't get my thoughts in order. Nothing would come out of my mouth; I literally couldn't speak. All I could do was keep my eyesight from blurring over. The nurses were persistent with their questioning; they kept grilling me in hopes of bringing me back into the world. The questions became a nuisance for all I could feel at that time was an overwhelming horrific burning inside of me. It was a sickness that was completely alien. I was so violently ill that I was rushed into the I.C.U.

The reason for my sickness was a result of a number of difficult challenges the surgeons encountered. There were three doctors involved in the surgery: two acting interventional neuro-radiologists and the head neurosurgeon. The procedure was complicated from the start due to the fact the aneurysm had grown significantly since the last procedure. Evidently, the surgeon's first attempt at securing the growth failed. Deciding that the task was too risky, they chose to stop then and there. They went to the overseeing neurosurgeon and informed him that they couldn't execute the procedure. The doctors also let their superior know that they had lost a coil in the process so they had to retrieve it before problems occurred. Understandably, the head physician wasn't happy with the news.

The doctors regrouped and with the guidance of the head neurosurgeon, they formed another strategy to tackle the complex procedure. Hours of delicate operation passed, but yet again, their attempt at sealing the aneurysm failed. At that time the aneurysm could have begun to seep blood into my brain, which may have led to my death. The situation was severe and my life was hanging by a thousand tiny coils. The doctors needed yet another consultation with their head neurosurgeon. They went in for a third attempt and with God's divine guidance working through the mortal hands of my surgeons; they were able to rectify my condition. Finally…. my aneurysm was secured.

Throughout the process the doctors used a certain radio-opaque dye agent necessary to capture the aneurysm's structure on film. It was an agent that didn't agree with me and set out to punish my body. After the surgery I was wheeled from the O.R. to the I.C.U. as the burning within my body immediately started. A frantic vomiting and heaving spell started, one that I couldn't stop. The on-slot of dark liquid spewing from within was almost too much for me to handle. That terrible sickness, some soft voices and many blurred lights are my only memories following my surgery. I became incoherent and passed out from the pain.

When I came to I found myself in the I.C.U. and within the cold confines, I experienced twelve hours of pain and suffering that I hope no one ever feels. I vomited and dealt with shooting pains and spasms in my back. My head felt like someone was inside trying to get out. My eyes were filled with a pressure that felt like an atom bomb was about to go off. All I could think was there must have been some kind of horrific demon inside of my brain who was taking over from the inside out. I remember telling myself, "I can't give into this now.... Just fight, fight with everything you have. This is your chance to show everyone that you choose life!!! There could be no other option but to kick the aneurism's ass."

The nurses had never seen such a negative reaction to a surgery; they actually had to console my sister at one point in time. Nurses desperately tried to administer drugs that would help squelch my pain and reduce vomiting. I can remember being in awe of Bernadette's strength and fortitude, as she stayed glued to my side the entire time. I believe I only survived because of the never-ending support of her and my brother.

It was around 5 a.m. when the vomiting of dark spew and spasms subsided. I could finally find some sleep in that night of a painful merry-go-round. When I woke it was 10 a.m. and around my bed swarmed several people; they buzzed like bees – darting left and right while trying to get a better look at me. The head surgeon was present and although I was in a haze the entire time I remember him being tall and slender. However, he was curt in the approach he used with me! When he spoke each and every one of his injections was piercing and to the point. He was all work and absolutely no play. A bit of levity in that instance could have helped, but he pushed on and began to bombard me with small tasks and questions. I came to realize that he was just doing his job in that he had to test me both mentally and physically.

"Raise this hand!" he ordered. I could barely do it but found some strength and responded by raising my right hand.

"Follow my finger!" he said. Fortunately I was able to do so. The doctor was putting me through quick directives that I strictly followed.

When the routine began to slow down the doctor said, "I hear you had a bit of a challenge last night."

My sister chimed in quickly, "Oh yeah she did!" Bernadette then explained what transpired.

He turned, looked at my sister and said, "Quit babying her!"

The look on my sister's face was certainly one I didn't think she was capable of. I believe that if Bernadette could have sucker punched him she just might have.

The Dr. continued, "Look, she hasn't eaten and she needs some nourishment so I've ordered her something. Once she's eaten I want her to get up, out of bed and dressed. Then you can take her back to your hotel room to get some rest. I will see Mary once more tomorrow then you will be able to take her home. She will then follow up with Dr. Miller in Jacksonville."

My sister and I thought he must be kidding. Not only were we mortified by his comments but it seemed his fellow colleges were taken aback as well. The two doctors that actually performed the procedure began to speak out to challenge those stern orders; however, their efforts were shut down immediately.

He concluded to announce to the room, "She's fine. She'll be ready to go home tomorrow."

The swarm of suits and ties in my room turned to go. My sister and I were dumbfounded and forced to find the strength to adhere to the doctor's instructions. It was imperative that I get up, out of bed and back into the swing of life. Well, that's exactly what we did. I felt the doctor's urgency and was consumed with a burst of energy that filled my spirit with determination. I realized the evil man who I felt was callous and cold-hearted, was being that way only because it was necessary for me to move forward without hesitation. I understood he believed in what he was doing: it was his demanding way that propelled me from my bed and back into life.

I respect the method he chose when dealing with my most complicated situation and I also thank him. It made me appreciate Dr. Miller and Mary's bedside manner even more. I couldn't wait to get back into their care.

The next morning the plan continued and I was transported from the hospital via wheelchair. As I glided down the ramp I began to cry. The revelation that I was "fixed" was sinking into my soul. I was alive and my eyesight was intact: Halleluiah! I sobbed tears of joy while I lovingly grasped the hands of my brother and sister. The surgery was a success and I was now living a miracle. I looked to the heavens and thanked God, my creator.

After a few days Bernadette and I headed for home. As we made our way through the airport I found myself limping a bit; but no worries, I was all smiles and filled with happiness. We talked about many of the choices that were made throughout that miraculous journey. It was agreed: perhaps the best choice anyone made was to trust in the dynamic team that was Nurse Mary and Dr. Miller. Without their love and courage I fear for what my outcome might have been. Dr. Miller displayed a courageous act of valor by stepping back and removing any ego he had in order to allow other surgeons to perform the surgery... Now that was an incredible blessing. I know I wouldn't be here today if Nurse Mary and my favorite doctor hadn't been steadfast in convincing me to go to Minnesota for that life saving surgery. These special people don't ask for accolades and yet they go about their daily lives performing miracles. That's truly what sets them apart. I love them both and we're close friends to this day. My family and I now stand and give you the glorious ovation that you two deserve. I would have it no other way.

What I Have Gained

To never give up in life is a stance that can only be found through undying faith. This commitment, to never give up, is easier said than done. It is a conviction that comes from the soul and it can't be taught; it's a mind-set that is grown from a seed within. It was only after reflecting on my wonderful life that I knew, subconsciously, that I needed to come out swinging in order to save my existence. There were too many important factors in my life to just wait for the inevitable. The choices I made after being told I had no further options, led me to meet the angels who paved the path for the cure. Those choices were undoubtedly life changing.

End of ACTS III.

INNER MISSIONS

The following missions are personal values from ACTS III that I embrace.

Acceptance: To take direction from the heart (instead of my head).

Choices: Never give up.

Truth: Face my fears head-on.

Sharing: Show unconditional love to my children every day.

ACTS
PART IV

Henry's Swan Song

When I was two years old my dad, the crooner, would sing to me as he bounced me up and down on his knee. I loved listening to him sing, especially when he belted out one of my favorite songs: "A Pretty Girl". His voice was incredible and with each vibrant note I became more and more mesmerized. Dad always looked directly into my eyes just so that I would feel like I was the only person sitting in the audience. Not only was my dad a bubbly entertainer, but he also loved teaching his musical skills to others just as much as he enjoyed performing. I remember a very special day when dad had just finished belting out a great rendition of "A Pretty Girl". He looked down at me and said, "Mary, I'm going to teach you some of my favorite songs so that when you grow up we'll be able to sing together." My eyes lit up in sparkles of cheshire and my smile radiated from pure excitement.

In no time at all I learned many of the classic songs. "I Left My Heart in San Francisco", "Won't You Come Home Bill Bailey", "Love" and many others (every time I think of those songs I know dad is right here with me). One favorite tradition of ours was singing a silly song at the end of each of our lessons. My dad would say, "O.K. Mary. Now you have to get down but before you do…" Then I would always end his sentence by saying, "Yes dad. Now sing the song, 'I Went to the Animal Fair'".

If you've never heard the song, it goes a little something like this:

I went to the animal fair

The birds and bees were there

The big baboon by the light of the moon

Was combing his auburn hair

The monkey he got drunk

Climbed up the elephant's trunk

The elephant sneezed, ha-chew! And fell on his knees

So what became of the monk, the monk, the monk?

Every time we sang that silly, song dad would bounce me up and down on his knee; that always made me feel like I was on the world's best teeter-tooter. When the song was finished I shimmied down from his knee as we both laughed like little kids. Dad always pulled me close, cheek-to-cheek, so that he could give me big hugs and kisses before bed (oh, and a little whisker burn). Playfully, as if he had just performed before a grand audience at The Lincoln Center, dad would say, "**Thank you, thank you, thank you**".

I think it's easy for people to become sheltered by the daily pleasures life gives us. Therefore, it's common and very easy to fail to recognize that death is riding right along with us. I'm sure there are times when we all take life for granted. I was at death's door with every passing medical procedure I had to endure and one false step would have certainly cemented my destiny. That experience thrust my eyes wide opened – so wide in fact that I now see the world in different ways.

A few years before I was treated for my aneurysm dad was diagnosed with cancer for the second time. Understandably, the news hit hard and devastated my family. As children our subconscious teaches us to believe that our parents are invincible. We see them as "superheroes" that will be with us forever. Children have that special innocence that allows them to believe in the word 'forever'. The word is used in fairytales and repeated on television, 'forever' is everywhere. When I learned of my dad's pancreatic cancer, the security I felt when I thought of "forever" quickly faded away.

The doctor's first order of business was to insert a shunt into his body in order to redirect superfluous bile. To our amazement and relief, my superhero passed the test with flying colors. He had lived four comfortable years after the diagnosis and that surgery, but then the cancer returned and attacked him with a ruthless conviction. My family and I witnessed first-hand how gruesome and relentless cancer can be. I walked into dad's hospital room and all I could do was focus on the complicated maze of tubes that protruded from his fragile body. The machines warbled as they made ominously stale and intimidating sounds. I was unnerved and panicked as I tried to wrestle with the brutality of seeing my father in such a painful condition. Right then, I realized we were all in for a fight.

When the battle started my family and I decided to set a full-proof plan in place. The first leg of the plan was to have someone constantly at dad's bedside, no matter what the hour of the day or what the visitor's rules were... someone would be there. We also made sure to log everything that was happening with him so as to help and alert the nurses of any new developments. My work schedule allowed for me to spend time at the hospital in the evenings. I can remember many sleepless hours sitting by my father's side holding his hand softly in mine just to let him know he wasn't alone. Being the avid music lover that my father was, my family made sure that he didn't go an instant without some of his favorite tunes. Dad would smile in gentle appreciation as I sang one of his favorites, a song that he taught me himself: "I Left my Heart in San Francisco". I sang to him throughout the midnight hours while the pale tranquil moonlight blanketed us with peace and hope.

After some very tough and exhausting days the doctors were finally able to alleviate my father's pain a little. As the pain subsided he regained a little bit of his appetite which gave the doctors the go ahead to remove some of the tubes that helped my father's food intake. Although he appeared to be regaining strength, the battle had taken its toll. So against all odds I forced myself to accept the fact that my superman was in decline. We knew how sick my father was so after talking with hospital staff we knew it was best that dad be moved to a hospice facility. There, they could see to it that he received the best treatment available. We were all familiar with the hospice facility because he had received care there before (that last time, he beat the odds and recovered). The center was the perfect place for dad in so many ways. Above everything else, my family loved how their staff always treated patients just like family.

Although we didn't speak of it much, everyone understood the hospice would be where my dad took his first steps toward a heavenly paradise. Therefore, I wanted to spend every possible moment with him so I made sure to ride in the ambulance to assure dad that he wasn't alone.

"Are you there?" dad would ask repeatedly.

I reassured him, "Yes, dad. I'm right here next to you."

Like every loving daughter who adores her father, I refused to believe the ride was leading to an end. If you have never ridden in an ambulance while the person you love lay next to you, I can assure you it's a frightening and painfully existential experience. When we arrived at the hospice facility the nurses took extra care to sufficiently examine my father's condition. Shortly thereafter, the head nurse took me aside.

Softly, she said, "Mary, it's my opinion that your father may only have a few days left to live."

The words punctured my heart like a nasty dagger of reality because it forced me to understand that my father wouldn't be with me forever. The light and energy of my spirit was steamrolled in seconds flat: I was lost. The first night I laid next to my father as he rustled uncomfortably while calling my name out into the darkness... just to make sure I was there. On occasion he asked that I lay my soft cheek on his warm chest while we held hands in our eternal father-daughter love. He was lucid during the first night and I made sure to hold his hand tight as we shared intimate conversations. Repeatedly, I expressed how great of a husband, father, and grandfather he was to his entire family.

Though his medication didn't appear to have severe side effects I often found dad drifting off to distant places. When he floated away I listened to conversations he had with his deceased family members. It sounds strange but during those talks he sought out his siblings and also found his parents somewhere in his journey. I was literally sent into a whirling trance as I felt that we were all in the same room sharing an infinite love. Then, as though nothing had happened, my dad returned to reality and began talking to me again.

After several hours of sporadic conversation dad was finally able to get some much needed rest. I slipped away from the hospice center to head home, I needed to freshen up and regain my composure. When I returned to the hospital I was surprised to see my entire family, including my mom, surrounding my father's bed with a radiant love. Seeing my mom instantly boosted my spirits and reminded me that no one is ever... ever alone (especially Henry). Bernice, the lovely nurse, had been by her husband's side for 72 years. She knew that very moment might be the most special and important time they would ever share. The Crooner and the Nurse came together: it was to be the Crooner's Swan Song.

When people passively mention the phrase, 'the more the merrier', I instantly try to illustrate just how powerful that statement is. I let people know just how special our loved ones are, and when I entered my dad's room that all too familiar phrase didn't do this family gathering justice. I remember the powerful feeling that rushed through me, one that must have been orchestrated by God. It was truly a day filled with beautiful love. As I slowly made my way to my father's bedside, I gave warm and tender hugs to each of my family members. When I reached my dad's side something was amiss because we all noticed that his breathing had become somewhat labored and complicated. I was instantly hit with another harsh brick of reality – I again realized that my father was slipping away. At that moment, all we wanted to do was comfort dad in any way we could. My family decided to do the one thing that came natural to all of us, we sang to our father. In unison, we stood side by side and belted out every one of dad's favorite ballads. His birthday was coming up in the next month so we decided to blast out a colorful rendition of "Happy Birthday". From there we moved on to sing our father's most beloved Christmas carols.

Standing gently hand-in-hand as we sang, each of us reached down into the depths our soul to find something extra special in our voice – a little something extra just so that our father would know how much we loved him and at that moment in life, everything was for him and him alone.

My family wasn't aware of it but some of the nurses had swarmed around the room to listen to us sing. Some of them were even so kind as to say how powerful and uplifting it all was; telling us they'd never seen such a loving tribute (one lovely nurse even went so far as to say she thought we were angels singing from heaven).

Dad was visibly growing weaker as the hours passed so we stayed vigilant and made sure to keep our spirits high. Time was more valuable than ever. Therefore, my brother Gary decided to sing to his father —he realized that it might be a final loving tribute so he softly sang one of dad's favorites: "Oh Danny Boy". My brother's soothing and beautiful voice filled everyone's heart with a numbing, peaceful tranquility. The performance encompassed Gary's musical brilliance and it was certainly the best I'd ever heard him perform. I looked around the hospital room and quickly realized that there wasn't a dry eye to be spied. The tears flowed like uninterrupted waves. When Gary finished singing I found myself overwhelmed with admiration. Picture if you will, a son standing before his dying father as he somehow finds an inner-warrior to help convey his majestic love and admiration through music. I couldn't comprehend how difficult it must have been to find the strength to perform for dad one last time. I just couldn't – but I was about to find out.

Immediately after Gary finished his song, a nurse made her way in to check on dad's vital signs. With one slight gesture she let us know that his time might be near: we instantly felt the serious and inevitable situation that now lay before us. As a family, we decided the best thing to do was to let our hero know that he was surrounded by love. As I stood on one side of the bed, Bernadette stood closely on the other. Mom laid her head gently on my father's chest and our entire family softly began to pray. In unison and as a loving tribute, we said the "Our Father".

Shortly after finishing the tear jerking prayer, I could feel my sister's eyes fixed on me. She knew that I just wanted to shout and ask everyone, "So what's next? Where do we go from here?" My father's heartbeat was slowing to the point that it made me feel as if every passing second might be his last. Fear stung and stabbed at my heart because I believed that I would never get to hear another of my dad's wonderful songs sung to me again. At that point, Bernadette (my rock) gave me a reassuring look that told me it wasn't dad's time to go yet... not yet. Suddenly, an electric feeling coursed its way through my hand as I placed my hand on his chest – relishing in his powerful warmth. I instantly knew it was my father's heart fighting to pass his great love on to us one last time. Sadly, as God made it so, there wasn't another loving heartbeat to follow. God chose to help my father transition to his next life and allowed his family to say goodbye with our most profound love.

I was in shock so I reached out to my family, hugging them and telling them how much I loved them. We all bowed our heads and cried as we prayed. My family asked the good Lord to cradle our father in his loving arms just as our dad had cradled us for so many wonderful years. I prayed that dad's passing was as comfortable as God could possibly make it. My mother peacefully laid her entire body across her husband as she softly said goodbye.

"I love you Henry. I love you so much and I always will," she said.

At that moment the reality of the situation blasted me with a chilling sadness. I had to find strength. At the time, looking to my mother was all I had to do because she had always taught me the true meaning of absolute fearlessness, faith and love. At that moment I believe I admired my mother more than ever. St. Bernice embraced an entire family by dedicating her life to her beloved Crooner: Henry, that whimsical musician who captured her heart all those years ago.

My father's passing was like watching the main supportive pillar of a great monument being washed away. Needless to say, a celebration was in order and one fit for a King. After taking time to power through the pain and the river of tears, my family and I wanted to plan a ceremony that would highlight my father's passion for music. I knew the celebration had to convey how our dad always sang his way through life (let's just say it wasn't going to be easy). How could we encompass a lifetime of music, laughter and love all in one celebration? How could we even start planning?

The LaCroix clan, as a unit, put its heart to the grindstone to make sure we created a fitting memorial for our father. We wanted it to be a celebration that would hopefully be one dad labeled, **"One for the books"**. My family felt comfortable by either singing or giving a tribute in church. I can't speak for other members of my family but on the day of the memorial I was shaking like a November leaf being harassed by a frigid wind. I sensed we were all nervous and very anxious before entering church that day because it would be the last performance in front of our super hero. As each of dad's children took center stage to say goodbye, it was clear that his friends and family were deeply moved by our tributes. The songs were powerful and the heartfelt words expressed just how much we loved him. Without pointing it out, everyone could feel that dad was listening as he smiled his shining smile.

As for me, my nerves were working overtime before I went up to sing (my mom picked out a song for me to sing to dad, especially from her). As I made my way to the microphone I looked down and noticed that my hands were shaking ever so slightly. Emotion and electricity surged through my veins, but I knew I had to collect myself so I wouldn't disappoint my family. Above all else, I wanted to make my father happy. I regrouped and with my brother accompanying me on the piano I started to sing the song, "You Are So Beautiful". I reached deep and lovingly pulled the words from my heart as I looked at my mother who seemed to be in a sea of tranquility. She was sitting in the very first pew and it was like dad was right next to her holding her hand. As I continued to sing, I was overwhelmed with the feeling that I was singing directly to my father. It comforted me to know that he was listening as he peacefully rested just a few paces away. I made my way down the alter stairs to stand next to my mother; I wanted her to know that I was singing directly to both of them. It was if they both wanted me to sing the song to each other. I found my heart in that song and wanted to share it while I held her hand. It was all for her comfort and to assure our mother that she wasn't and would never be alone. Henry would always be right by her side.

At song's end, I remember feeling a great sense of gratitude for having the opportunity to express my love through music. I felt so peaceful that I leaned over and kissed my father as he rested. Then, I whispered goodbye to him in his ear. With tears streaming down my cheeks, I gave my mother a delicate yellow rose and a sweet kiss. I told her that they were ever lasting gifts from her loving husband. My mother adored yellow roses and they were always dad's favorite gift to her on every special occasion.

Holding the rose gently in her hand, my mother slowly made her way up to dad's casket. She wanted to give him one last gentle loving kiss and place the rose next to him. It was her way of letting him hold onto his favorite flower as he started a new and beautiful journey with God. Then, with an angel's breath, my mom softly whispered something in his ear. My mother later told me what she said, "Henry – hold on to this beautiful yellow rose… you had better because I will be looking for it when I come to find you as we start our next journey together."

My family began to find peace through prayer and music. Throughout the day I believe we all made the transition and accepted God's love. We gave into the belief that he would take great care of our adoring father. Thus, the ceremony came to an end.

When we exited the church a peaceful feeling blanketed my heart because I realized we had succeeded in giving our father the tribute worthy of a King. I knew that everyone felt the immense love that radiated from his soul. As our friends left the church they would say, "We thought it was amazing. God bless. Everything was beautiful. It was like we were at a concert that included everyone. Thank you."

I am blessed to have had such wonderful parents. Now that some time has passed, my gratitude and spiritual connection to them has soared higher than I ever thought possible. With a light heart, I always say that I couldn't have ordered better or more loving parents from the Spiegel catalog.

In my heart, I truly know that Henry would want to say something to his friends and family that said goodbye to him that day.

My superhero would say, "**Thank you! Thank you! Thank you!**"

We love you Dad!

My Awakening

A year had gone by after my father's passing and it was his uplifting spirit which gave me the strength to push through each and every day – I was back into the swing of things selling homes to people in paradise. Life was prone to spin my head on my shoulders because things had become extremely hectic; but it was in my busy schedule that I found the most comfort. I was a little jaded and unbeknownst to me, my work was all my life had become. There were days when I found it hard to interact with my co-workers and prospective clients: I just wanted to shut down. Most days I had to focus intently and put my heart to the grindstone just to make it through. After work I would usually retreat to my comfortable house that became my fortress of solitude. There, every night, I buried myself under the soft covers of my bed and found comfort in suppressing the painful feeling of losing my father. That warm shelter became a cocoon-like sanctuary where I could pray and speak to God.

I quietly put my feelings on the top shelf of my closet, tightly closed the door and hoped to lose them forever. My emotional closet wasn't a place I liked visiting but I loved hiding my feelings there. It was a secure vault for my troubles and above all else it provided me with the sense of being in complete control. Hiding my feelings was a new process for me. Throughout my life I always took pride in being a 'straight-forward' person and always made a point to let people know how I truly felt; that all changed after my father's death. For me, life became mostly about hiding and ignoring any and all painful emotions that tried to batter down my cement walls.

It was Thanksgiving weekend that year and my life was swarming with family members who were starting to celebrate. Thanksgiving, in particular, was one of my parent's most favorite days. I loved spending holidays with my family but that year, things were different. When turkey day approached I became just that, a turkey! I didn't want to socialize with anyone and just wanted to be left alone. My plan was to immerse myself in work and let my family enjoy the festivities for me.

That holiday I decided to work straight through the weekend and on Sunday the weather turned extremely gloomy. Once again, I decided to jump into bed so that I could escape the world. I instantly started to lick my wounds as I reflected on a year of painful drama. After some deep reflection I fell into a disheartened sleep then woke with an enormous hunger (the rumbling in my stomach was loud enough to wake my entire neighborhood). To make the matters worse I found myself walking into a kitchen full of empty cupboards (for anyone who knows me they'll say my kitchen usually consists of only bread and water). The wind and rain continued to whip throughout the area so the last thing I wanted to do was brave the elements just for the sake of food (I mean, for food's sake!). But my hunger persisted to grow and grow. I got into my car and headed to one of my favorite restaurants in paradise. At the time I didn't feel like being surrounded by too many people so I was relieved to find only a few other customers around. The wait staff already knew my favorite drink, a patron margarita sans salt, so I was good to go.

It is in my nature to avoid eye contact with strangers in public places, but in that restaurant and on that specific night, things felt different. After settling into my seat and taking that first sip of patron, in walked one of the most handsome men I have ever laid eyes on. As he walked to the bar to sit down the man knew he had caught my eye. I felt that I caught his attention as well (that's at least what I tell myself). As I nibbled on my food I couldn't stop laughing at a silly competition on the television. Two couples had to get a squid out of their partner's pants without using their hands and boy did it look squishy. As I laughed the handsome stranger caught my attention because he was laughing too. Our eyes met and an immediate and powerful connection shot through my heart.

Moments after that quick flirtation, Sue my waitress, came to me and said, "Hey Mary did you notice the guy at the bar?" It was common for the waitresses to try and fix me up.

"Of course I noticed him Sue. He's gorgeous," I quickly said. Sue and I had never seen the man before so we assumed he was from out of town.

She leaned over and whispered in my ear, "I think he's single. I didn't notice a ring on his finger."

Then I did something I had never done in my life. I asked my gracious waitress if she would do a little reconnaissance and ask if he was single; and most importantly, if I could buy him a drink. Shortly thereafter I saw him get up and leave. Shoot! I didn't think Sue had the chance to ask him anything and was afraid he simply paid his bill and went on his way. With a sullen mood, I turned my attention back to my delicious margarita (my friend). I looked up and suddenly there he was, standing right next to me.

"I hear you want to buy me a drink?" the handsome man said.

I was shocked and somewhat bowled over, I literally didn't know what to say.

"Well yes, I'd like to buy you a drink. If you're single, that is. Are you?" I asked.

"I'm as single as the day is long. And you?" he asked.

I said, "I certainly am."

With a smile stretching from ear-to-ear he asked me for permission to sit down. The first thing I did was tell him that it wasn't normal for me to approach men I wasn't familiar with. Most importantly, I absolutely didn't want him to get the wrong idea and think it was something I did often. There was just something about him, something very alluring.

I said, "I don't want you to get the wrong idea."

"Well, I hope this isn't common for you. I'm hoping that it's special," he said gently.

All I could think at the time was: this guy was good! After we made a crack in the ice he formally introduced himself by kindly extending his hand to me. Patrick was his name. We softly shook hands and we both sensed that something special was in the air.

The first question that came out of my mouth was, "Where the heck did you come from?"

He answered, "I'm returning from my parent's home in Atlanta. There was an accident on the expressway so I decided to take a break and get something to eat."

The restaurant was far from the expressway so I wondered how we ended up in the same place (he admitted to me that he was a little lost). I didn't think he was lost at all and I thought he was in the right place at the right time.

The conversation we started could have lasted an eternity. Everything was so easy with him. Patrick told me he lived and worked in West Palm Beach, FL as a helicopter pilot and trainer. He was in the middle of changing jobs to work for the State Department. In the upcoming months Patrick told me he would be working as a subcontractor flying helicopters in Iraq. Yes – he was leaving for Iraq. Iraq! I was disheartened by the news because for me to have such a strong connection with someone, that quickly, was very rare. I was understandably disappointed but it also excited me.

The last thing I wanted to do was put a damper on our short meeting so it was best to just go along with everything. Patrick and I had a great time getting to know each other; so great that hopes of some future dates began to arise. We finished our drinks and decided to exchange phone numbers. As we walked to our cars, he turned to open his door, leaned down and gave me a kiss.

I was beside myself (nicely surprised really). It was one of the boldest things a man has ever done with me and was absolutely one of the best kisses I ever had. All I could feel was the electricity vibrating through the air.

"That was nice," I said.

He laughed for a bit and could tell I wasn't used to moving so fast; next, he wanted to gauge my reaction. I felt comfortable with him from the time we met eyes so I was certainly all right with the kiss. Most men might have been ready for a right hook to the jaw in that type of situation, but in that scenario everything was flowing forward. It was difficult to do but Patrick and I said our goodbyes then parted ways. I felt like I was sailing on a sea of silk.

It astounds me how a simple choice like getting out of bed led me to meet such a dynamic and wonderful person (did I mention he was handsome?). Choices can take you on wonderful journeys that you thought were impossible. All it takes is one choice and your world can be changed forever.

A week after meeting the lost pilot I was back into my daily work routine and things were rolling smoothly. Then, the phone rang. It was Patrick. He surprised me with the "shock-and-awe" approach that I had heard about. I was ecstatic that he'd called and we commenced to jabber on for a while like a couple of old friends. He kept telling me how much he enjoyed our brief time together and hoped to meet again.

The art of conversation can get lost in today's mixed maze of technology; but the talks that I had with Patrick were always better than any zeros and ones could ever produce. Looking back, I realize how comforting and uplifting it was to talk with someone so dedicated to his career. I learned that Patrick spent many years in the military, in the Army to be specific. After years of flying Patrick returned to civilian life and started a new path as a flight instructor. After hearing his thrilling stories I was always left feeling exhilarated and wanting more. After weeks of great phone calls, Patrick and I had become extremely close. We shared everything and as time went on it became more difficult for me to grasp the fact that he was leaving for Iraq. It was something I knew I would have to deal with in the future. Patrick told me that he was also in the reserves and had to spend a weekend of training in Tampa (which is only an hour's drive from paradise). I knew his life was in constant flux so I quickly accepted his invitation to meet him there.

That weekend in Tampa was everything I hoped it would be. Our time together flowed as easily as clouds float through a beautiful blue sky. It seemed like we danced and laughed the entire time and I can remember that I wanted the clock to stop so we could have all the time we wanted. The chemistry between us was explosive; so intense that I knew it was something like no other. The idea of being open to an intimate relationship hadn't crossed my mind in a long time (I felt that it just wasn't in the cards), but at that moment my eyes were wide open. Still being somewhat closed off because of my father's passing and just like most people I had a previous relationship that didn't end well: so I was extremely hesitant to put my heart out there once again. My heart was locked away and shielded from emotional distress.

The magical white sandy weekend ended so we had to say our goodbyes. We kept up our phone conversations and grew even closer as time moved forward. Patrick let me know he wouldn't be able to speak with me as often when he was in Iraq. Now came the time for me to deal with his choice to risk his life in the military. His decision reminded me that we must be cognizant that our decisions not only affect us, but they have the capacity to impact those around us. Patrick's choices were beginning to have an effect on my life and I realized it. I was comfortable with his career choice, but others I didn't understand.

Quickly, I had to accept that he was willing to put himself in harm's way. I also had to accept the 'unique' way in which he dealt with his romantic relationships. As our friendship grew it was apparent that Patrick was accustomed to getting into the routine of dating several women at once. With so much random travel and a sporadic work schedule, it was just a life that he had adapted to. He was always honest about his situation and assured me that he would understand if I didn't want to be a part of his life in that way any longer. It may seem difficult to grasp, but I didn't judge the life he led or how he dealt with relationships. Thus, I was faced with an important choice of my own. I had to ask myself: do I push for a traditional relationship and risk my friendship with him? Or, do I accept the current state of our relationship and let things play out?

I decided to set aside my thoughts for having a traditional relationship and take the road less traveled. I thought, "Who knows? Maybe there is something to be learned here". I believe that Patrick is not only handsome but that he demands attention because of the fascinating charisma and personality he possesses. When he walks into a room he has a presence like no other: I call it the x-factor. It wasn't a difficult choice to let myself be open to his somewhat chaotic lifestyle because he constantly kept me on edge with his great magnetic energy. I felt the decision was best for the both of us in that we could salvage a true spiritual relationship.

The dark day arrived when my pilot had to take flight for Iraq. Duty called and he was off to serve his country for the next two months. After, he would return for a month's leave. Being the dedicated and honorable man he is, Patrick decided to volunteer for an additional month of service. That bowled me over because he did it just so others who were there longer could be with their families.

Three months of spotty telephone conversations were laid out before us. Adjusting to his absence was heart wrenching and I quickly realized that it was the first time I was in a relationship with a military man. Therefore, the idea of combat and the possibility of death were new to me. I said prayers for him and asked God to watch over my brave soldier during his flying missions over Iraq. I prayed that God would keep him safe.

During the next three months our relationship morphed into one big emotional phone call. We talked often and he made it a priority to keep me posted as to his safety when time allowed. Each time we talked I wanted to reach out and hug him simply to let him know how much I cared.

Patrick's zest for life is next to none and his inquisitive nature rivals that of a child. He is always asking questions and waits sincerely for someone's answer in hopes of getting to learn more about them. His passion for travel has taken him around the globe to some destinations that might amaze people. It wouldn't be possible to do what Patrick does with a weak mind or a faint heart. He's constantly put to the test and somehow always seems to cope with any challenge that is presented.

There are two 'extremes' of my handsome stranger's personality. On one side he is boldly confident when putting his life in danger for the better good. On the other side, his more personal side, there is a level of equal vulnerability. Through our long distance conversations I learned that it was because of this vulnerability that he needed several relationships in his life at once. Never wanting to be alone, he felt that by surrounding himself by as many people as possible, it would ensure that he could avoid any chance of loneliness. If one person exited his life there was always someone there to fill that spot.

I understood his position: no one ever really wants to be alone (that's my opinion). I may not have wholeheartedly agreed with his choices, but how could I determine what was best? I realized if there was such a person to do so it certainly wasn't me. I struggled with his choices because our outlook and viewpoints on relationships are totally opposite. Concerning my romantic relationships, I've usually had a difficult time opening up and allowing people into my life. Patrick, on the contrary, opened my eyes in so many ways. Our relationship has spanned a period of four years and was completely different from any other I'd experienced. For the majority of our relationship he was traveling back and forth from Iraq. That crazy traveling schedule left little time for his personal relationships. But Patrick always went to great lengths just to spend time with his loved ones when on leave. It goes without saying that balancing that type of relationship was difficult. Although he was running here and there to be with family and friends, we always made time for each other and our friendship.

Patrick and I were blessed to spend an entire week together in Florida and during that vacation we hit some of my favorite spots. One of those hot spots is a fabulous hotel in Orlando. Anytime I'm in that area I try to make a point to swing by even just to soak up the ambiance. During our stay we acted like the usual suspects and spent the hot days cooling off at the pool. Always the joker, Patrick would surprise me by picking me up in his strong arms and send me flying. One specific time he simply picked me up and cradled me in his arms. I instantly felt a sense of peace and comfort sooth my soul. I finally found the strength to ask him something that was gnawing at my conscious.

I asked, "Patrick, if my mother decides to leave this earth in the near future, will you make sure you come home to be with me? No matter where you are in the world, will you make the effort to be here?" (To this day I'm not sure why I asked that question. Looking back, I don't feel it was because of my mother. She was fine at the time.)

Mom cared for Patrick dearly. I knew his presence in her time of need would mean the world to her (and me). I knew that I would need my friend's strong shoulders and loving support during that time.

He didn't flinch and said, "I don't care if I'm in Iraq or traveling the world. I promise. I will drop everything and come to be by your side."

During that week we grew close and recognized that our relationship had reached a new plateau. Our connection was stronger than ever and I loved it. Oh no – I spoke too soon. The very next month Patrick dropped a bomb on my heart.

"I've decided to go with my reserve unit to Afghanistan. I need to if I want to get my full retirement plan," he abruptly said.

I was stunned and just stared at him.

I will have to go to Afghanistan for about a year to qualify."

My heart and mind were unsteady while I sat silently trying to absorb everything. It was hard to process: the idea of the man I had grown so close with was dedicating himself to such a dangerous life. Just like most bombs, another was about to fall from the sky. Immediately after I learned he was going to Afghanistan, Patrick bluntly told me that he had met someone else. Just like that, he decided it was time to commit to a relationship (with someone else). Although we understood our relationship was open, I couldn't wrap my head around why he chose that particular time to change his approach.

Our friendship included the usual 'intimate factor' that most close relationships do. Even though the intimacy was nice, it was the connection that Patrick and I developed over the years that was most important to me. Our alliance is what ultimately mattered most. I was hurt and cemented in my tracks when the words escape from his mouth. I didn't have an answer ready for that meaningful situation so I paused and thought of how to handle everything. A mature and spiritual response was my best bet; however, underneath it all it crushed my heart.

Like a mature adult and not a baby kaka-face, I chose to accept Patrick's choice and wished him well. Honestly, I did love him and I still do. We both know that our unconventional relationship has been judged by many people; including family and friends. They have failed to understand its spiritual foundation. To this day it is still difficult to explain but we get each other and feel connected in so many ways. It was so simple and easy to accept each other's differences and to just love one another throughout all of life's painful challenges. Ultimately, we refuse to judge each other. To those in close relationships I can say that it's critical to accept your loved one's 'uniqueness' completely. That trait is very rare and essential if a friendship is going to last.

In regards to his decision to commit to another woman, I will admit that I'm puzzled as to why he didn't choose me. These days I understand that it was God's path for Patrick to follow and ultimately, he chose to do so. Although it may be painful I will stand by my friend's side anytime he needs me and there will come a time when I can ask this question, "Why wasn't I the one?" I must also ask myself, "Do I deserve a man like Patrick? Do I deserve

something different? Not something better, just different?"
I've done some soul searching and truly believe that I am a
person worthy of something incredible. We all deserve to
be in a monogamous relationship and to be with one very
special person.

Monogamy is a gift that God has given to us and I
feel it must grow from the foundation of a great friendship.
When the inevitable rough and tumble times roll through
life, a solid friendship will shine through any cloudy sky.
I've learned that lesson through the many powerful
friendships I've been fortunate enough to forge over the
years. If my relationship with Patrick hadn't started out as
romantically as it did, the end result might have been
different. Without the intimacy he might have seen me
more as a friend and known I'm capable of giving
unconditional love.

When people decide to express their love for
someone, we're accepting everything about that person:
individual choices included. I accepted my pilot and all of
his individual choices without question. During that
relationship I was faced with diverse challenges that I

made sure to hold close to my heart. My handsome stranger was always there to offer his loving support and it proved to be an experience like no other.

Bravery and generosity are worthy of great love and my pilot was chalk full of both virtues. I've witnessed a countless number of people thanking Patrick for his military service and self-sacrifice. After all of the countless accolades he has received, he still remains humble. I'm certain that God has a great love for that soaring pilot.

You will never know how straining it was for me to write about this special relationship. But I did and there it is, plain and simple. I reminisce about the night we met and it reinforces how fortunate I am to have someone like Patrick in my life. He opened my eyes to a variety of new ideas and different ways of looking at the world. For that, I thank him dearly.

Hopefully time will allow us to speak while he is in Afghanistan. I ask God to protect Patrick and shield him from harm. You will see what a great man and friend he is to me when you read a little further. The story hasn't ended just yet...

Look to the Sons

My life is similar to the popular television show of the early 1960's: "My Three Sons". I have three beautiful boys who have their own unique glow that guides me through every day. One of my major challenges in writing this book was deciding how and when to write about my boys. I now feel it's the perfect time to share the love and joy they bring me (whether they like it or not!). To begin with, without a doubt, they are my greatest gifts; they have always struck me as being cool young men. Over the next few pages I'll attempt to shed a glimmer of light on just how important they are to me (all the while trying to respect their privacy).

I have mentioned that Nathan is my first-born child (the name actually means 'gift'). From the time Nathan was a young boy, it was apparent that he had a strong sense of self and possessed an ease of confidence. The dedication and commitment to his life design is unparalleled mainly because Nathan focuses on demonstrating an inquisitive spirit. I learned of that inquisitiveness when my little guy did something truly adorable at the tender age of three.

One afternoon Nathan decided to pick up the phone and call his grandparents on his father's side. After figuring out the process all by his lonesome, needless to say, his extremely surprised grandparents had a fun and heartwarming talk. From then on my fearless adventurer knew how to talk to his grandma and grandpa whenever he desired. Nathan became such a phone-techie that he started to call other family members as well just to spread some youthful love. I loved it (except for the phone bills! Luckily China wasn't on the speed-dial).

Nathan adored both sets of his grandparents and still holds the crown as the only little soldier who could tolerate the bellowing snores of grandpa Hank. Nestled nice and neatly next to my father, Nathan somehow found a melodic peace in the snoring as they both slept soundly. It was adorable to watch but as time played out I learned that my little man had an ulterior motive. My father was an avid fisherman and would wake up early to head out to the lake almost every morning. Nathan began to see the pattern so he would place his hand on grandpa's back so as to be woken by any sudden movement. Needless to say, grandpa and Nathan became great fishing buddies.

One powerful characteristic of Nathan's is his dedication to the well being of friends and family. It's a conviction that often gets him into hot water in his relationships because he can be somewhat overbearing – thus, but only sometimes, he comes off as being a bit controlling (sounds just like a mother). Just ask his brothers about the powerful attention he gives to his loved ones. However, when you peel away all of his tightly wrapped layers you learn there is much more beneath the surface.

From an early age Nathan was driven and had a vivacious spirit that could easily be seen in everything he did. When he first started school, my scholar was sure to prepare his school clothes for the next day. Nathan would meticulously lay them at the end of his bed each night in preparation. The funny thing about it was that he laid his outfits flat on the bed so he could see how it would look (something of a miniature mock-up). The avid student always followed his routine. I laugh when I think about those special times because he still diligently plans his days... always needing to know what's going to happen next.

Nathan and I went through the first four years of his life attached at the hip. We were without a doubt, best friends (BFs). We adored one another and knew we could talk about anything. I still remember Nathan's first day of kindergarten and how I had heard of the agonizing pain some parents felt when seeing their kids go off to school for the first time. When that big day came, I made sure to prepare myself. As usual, Nathan laid his clothes out and was ready for his new adventure (I recall thinking that he was going to just jump right into his clothes and take off running). The big morning arrived and to the bus stop we headed holding hands the entire way. As we were waiting for the bus, the other school children began to arrive as well. I could sense the other moms were filled with anxiety and apprehension just like I was. All of us were excited and terrified of that big yellow bus that was about to roll down the street and whisk our children away to the next chapter of their lives.

The bus arrived on time and to the disappointment of most parents we started to load our little soldiers for the big adventure. Nathan and I were at the back of the line and my heart was beginning to thump with vibrant anxiety. I realized the severity of the situation and everything was beginning to sink in: I literally started to hyperventilate. Now, for the more experienced parents out there, please keep in mind that it was my 'first day' of school. I didn't realize that I would be so overpowered with such gut wrenching emotions. Nathan was only four so shuttling him off was hard to do. As he took his first steps up the stairs my heart dropped something fierce and I could feel that all-too-familiar sinking feeling. When he reached the top step, Nathan turned around to look at me. I thought he might be frightened or he just didn't want to go – that would have been fine with me at the time.

Instead, he waved and said, "I love you mom."

I broke out in raindrop-sized tears (as I am now) and just stood frozen in my tracks. Nathan made his way to a seat and then he did something unexpected – he pressed his face to the window and started to blow me kisses. No!

Anything but that! As any mother can understand seeing a loving little gesture like that can melt you. The bus made its way down the road and disappeared. Quickly, I came to the realization that my little man was actually on the road to 'designing his own life'. I was heartbroken, not only because my son was starting a new life, but I was truly losing my best little buddy. Like a fool, I cried the entire way home. I found comfort in my tears throughout the rest of the day and by the time my little student came home my face was puffed up from all the sobbing.

He asked, "Mommy, are you sick?"

I replied, "No baby, mommy is just fine now."

Later that night I just kept asking myself, "How could this happen to me? I'm a strong person so how could one little day disrupt me so much? Why so many tears? Is this my 'mini-me'?"

It is easy for the parents out there who have been through similar situations to understand just how difficult those emotions can be. I can proudly say that the next day was easier for me, thank goodness! Although he was only four at the time, Nathan could sense how sad it made me to see him leave for school. In the future, my little angel always made sure to give me a big hug and kiss before he left.

As he grew up Nathan always played a major role in our family and proved to be a pillar of stability and strength. When he was seven his father and I decided to go our separate ways. That shift in our lives propelled Nathan to become more cognizant of what it was like to be a responsible adult. His brother Dean was only one at the time and we all quickly found ourselves on our own.

That was just the way life was going to be. In turn, my courageous trooper didn't waver and grew into a mighty warrior. As a young man Nathan seamlessly adapted to his adult-like responsibilities. By pure instinct he took on a fatherly persona for Dean and dedicated himself to his brother's well being. Once again, my 'gift' illustrated just how confident and responsible he was becoming.

Early on in life, however, there were the inevitable bumps and lumps in the road. On many occasions I could sense that Nathan desperately wanted to reach out and grasp his independence; with so many grown-up responsibilities laid on him, it was easy a toll being taken. Being somewhat of a control freak Nathan was creative and smart enough to design a system that gave him time not only for himself, but time to tend to his grown-up responsibilities. When it comes to a child's living situation, I feel that we can all agree it's an added perk to have your own bedroom while growing up. Well... Nate wanted his own space too but he kindly let his little brother sleep soundly next to him every night. My two little guys would also walk hand-in-hand to school every day; to me, they were all Kodak moments. Nathan, my little genius was hard at work.

Nathan and I endured many challenging times both spiritually and financially over the years. Thankfully he was the cutest 'time management officer' any mother could have hoped for.

When I decided to get married for the second time, Nathan was brave and graciously went with the flow. The most difficult aspect about it was that we would be packing up and moving our entire lives. Nathan was going from 7th into the 8th grade so it was difficult to uproot his life completely at that specific time. He was forced to leave behind some very close friends and ultimately a life that he was becoming accustomed to. With a cascade of heartfelt tears drowning our eyes, we left our hometown of Saginaw and made the hopeful trek to Brighton, MI.

I wasn't aware of the profound effect the move had on Nathan until he started to display some unusual behavior. That summer he immersed himself in books (mainly Stephen King novels) and rarely left his room. Although alarmed at first, I believed the reclusive behavior was just a phase and that with mostly everything else in life, time would mold the situation into a positive. I can say that it worried me most that Nathan might struggle to make new friends if he stayed held up in his room reading various morbid Stephen King novels (of all authors - Stephen King!). As time and many books passed, Nathan branched out and befriended a wonderful young man. The duo became quick partners in crime and over the next few years Nathan was running around with a number of new friends his own age. I could see that he was really maturing nicely and all the while I thought the 'big move' was a mistake.

After high school my wonderful son was accepted to Michigan State University so it was time to head off to college. I say in all selfishness, again, I had a horrific time adjusting to the fact that my first-born would be leaving the nest in order to spread his expanding wings. Yes, it was the first day of school all over again (I feel there should be a government issued rule that says parents should only have to endure the torture of seeing their kids off to school once!).

Nathan was an exceptional student at MSU. His main focus was criminology and he hoped to make the jump to law school one day. Things were going smoothly and after his junior year he began field studies at Georgetown University. The plan was playing out nicely; however, the other shoe was about to drop. On a return flight from Georgetown to Michigan, Nathan told me he was questioning his career path. Unbeknownst to me criminology and law were suddenly not high on his to-do-list. I couldn't believe what I was hearing and remember the sense of a slow burn starting to fuel a fire in my stomach. I tried to let my confusion fade and listen to his explanation (I thought— 'this had better be good'). Many parents feel that when our kids are at that pivotal age (an important span is 18 to 22), they usually don't have a clue as to what's at stake in regards to their future. Above all else, I was fronting the bill for Nate's education so the news smacked me like a Big Bertha golf club. The idea that really caught me off guard was my son's insistence that I should just accept the life altering news without questioning anything at all.

After the bomb dropped, I simmered down and tried on the outfit of an understanding parent. It took some time but I realized that the most important thing was Nathan's choice and why he was making the decision. I respected his brave heart in making such a bold choice. By putting his passion into action instead of just going along with something he didn't want, he ultimately avoided a huge mistake. I gained even more respect for Nate because he knew that dealing with a frantic and irate mother was inevitable! As he explained his decision, Nathan reassured me that he had done extensive research about the legal profession. To his dismay, unfortunately, it was a career path he couldn't see eye-to-eye with. He learned about the many situations attorneys must deal with on a daily basis, situations that Nate knew wouldn't fit him. Eventually, he came to terms with the idea that law wasn't going to be in his life's design.

I accepted my son's decision but only on one condition: I wanted to know what his concrete plan was for the future. For the rest of the plane ride Nathan explained some of his ideas and that he felt confident in some of them being successful. As I listened my subconscious gave way to the fact that all of my plans and goals I had had in mind for my son's career might not play out the way I had foreseen. It was necessary and some say crucial that I accepted any new path he wanted to take, and that's exactly what I did.

"You got it. Let's just finish out this year and then you can decide what your next steps will be. I will help you make it happen, whatever your plans are," I said reassuringly.

Looking back I feel that God came into action and stepped in to help me accept Nathan's choice. I always love when God steps in and makes his presence felt. I was powerfully out-voted so I started preparing for the next chapter of my son's life. Nathan spent the next year focusing on how he could possibly use the education he obtained at college to help him in life. How could I judge his decision? I could never muster up the courage to go to college, so I couldn't possibly understand what he was going through. Nathan and I will be by each other's side no matter what and can always put away the difficult circumstances that might fall in our path. When God blessed me with my brave soldier I was given one of the most incredible gifts possible: my Nate.

My middle son, Dean (or Deano, like his friends call him), is up next, front and center. From the second Dean opened his beautiful eyes to the world he was nothing short of an atomic blast of energy; it was like he was hooked to a battery charger and then cut loose on society when his gauge was set to red. He was upside-down and inside out before you could yell out his name. Dean's electricity came to Nathan's dismay for he was the one who had to harness most of the wild fires. To go along with a great energy, Dean proved to be extremely intelligent with a quick (sometimes too quick) and unmatched wit. The challenge for everyone was to get him to sit still long enough to put his smarts to the test. He was a kid of action, a miniature dare devil who loved to climb and push physical limits. There were times when I drank coffee straight through the night just to keep pace with Dean's insatiable appetite for intense action.

Those frantic days not only kept his blood racing, but there was a lot of vomiting on Dean's part that he had to endure. I guess that all of the running around and being upside-down would get to him once in a while. Needless to say Dean's ability to hold down the day's lunch wasn't his strong suit. It came to the point where I would just prepare myself for a good puking every time I'd pick the little guy up. It became such a game between Dean and I that he would hold off his spewing only to secretly ruin the backsides of some of my favorite business suits! (Oh, I just love my little boy so much!)

I cherished having the time to watch Dean race and navigate through his daily fun. Mainly, he stuck to his brother like velcro as the two would move as one whether it was a good or bad thing. Needless to say, the tight bond of brotherhood that grew between the two helped me manage them through some tough times.

Dean's intelligence started to shine brightly as he began school. I wanted to get him into the same school as Nathan because it was for gifted students and a place where I felt Dean could excel. He tested very well and passed the entrance exams with flying colors. Gaining entrance to the school was a gift, not only for its focus on academics but now Nathan and is little brother could walk to school together every day. Things were going really well but there was just one problem when it came to Dean and the classroom: he couldn't sit still! It wasn't long before the faculty realized that Dean was becoming a distraction to the other students. Ultimately, the time came when it was best for all parties to have Dean moved to a public school. I understood the situation and agreed to go along with the faculty's reasoning, but I soon realize that it was just the beginning of long path.

A few weeks had passed at Dean's new school when I was summoned for a parent-teacher conference. I thought to myself, "Oh no. Does he need to change schools again?" I learned quite the contrary; they wanted my little guy to move ahead two grades, not because of his behavior but because of his test scores. He was testing through the roof and was ahead of his grade so the teachers felt his energy and intelligence should be challenged even more. Needless to say, I was speechless and some confusion set in. I didn't understand how Dean could be pulled from one school because of his performance, and then advance forward two grades at the next. At the time I was against the idea because I didn't want Dean to be expected to keep up with children who were two years his senior – the pressure may have been a bit much. Therefore, I did the responsible thing and refused the recommendation and ultimately kept him with students who were his own age. In hindsight, it wasn't the best idea. It turned out that Dean was always a little ahead of the class and sometimes found it difficult to remain challenged. Transferring schools, having difficulty fitting in to his class, all of our sporadic moving, all of those factors made up a turbulent academic life for Dean. I certainly thought his life's path would be somewhat more difficult than the next kid's... I was wrong.

Dean always showed an immense love and dedication to our entire family. There was a phase of his childhood where I struggled to make ends meet in regards to money. Times were wickedly tough. When Dean was just four he learned the invaluable lesson of what money means. There was one specific week when I was attacked by a swarm of small but menacing disasters. In a matter days, both my washer and dryer completely broke down. Now that might not seem like Mt. Vesuvius had just erupted but for a woman trying to balance work, kids and financial obstacles, it was daunting. Shortly after I learned that I couldn't get my whites white, the refrigerator went on the fritz (yes, things do actually happen in 3's). The day before the fridge conked out on me I had just enough money to buy some milk for the kid's cereal. That morning, as we were all going through our fire-drill routine, I poured the milk onto the boy's cereal and was greeted with huge lumps of disgusting curdled milk (it was the sour-milk on the cake, if you will). I was at my wits end. No money, three broken appliances and two hungry boys: Oy veh!

I couldn't bear it and was saturated with desperation: I started crying. All I could do was to sit down at the dining room table, helplessly put my head in my hands and wait for the sky to fall. I felt hopeless and began to question everything in life. How could I raise my precious boys whom I loved so much with so little? As I wept I sensed a little body climbing up onto the table and sitting down in front of me; it was Deano. He sat in front of me with his legs crossed and then slid his hands under my face. With love, he slowly raised my face to his and looked into my eyes.

He told me, "It's alright mommy. I love you."

It may sound strange but I felt God was using my little Deano to speak to me. I was being told to stay strong and remain faithful. Quickly, I brushed aside the teardrops and gobble Dean up into one of the biggest bear hugs I've ever been given. Then I grabbed Nathan and hugged them both with everything my spirit had to offer. My boys whispered into my ear that it was O.K. for them to eat their beloved cereal without milk, that innocent and childlike sentiment brought more tears to my already swollen cheeks.

After the 'sour-milk' debacle the three of us were leaving the house when God truly showed his presence. I was emptying the pockets of a pair of jeans before washing them in the sink when I discovered a $20 bill! It was like striking oil or finding a sparkling gold brick (I quickly checked the back yard to see if there was a goose laying golden eggs). I gasped, showed the boys the money and suddenly like three crazed miners; we danced around the house in celebration. Yes, it was almost like we hit the jackpot or that we found a black bubbling crud in the ground. To our little family of three, that $20 bill was worth exactly that, one million. I learned a lesson from my boys that day. They taught me that not even the dourest of sour-milk could spoil **true family love**.

My boys proved to be warriors from the get-go. Dean has always had complications with his stepfather and sometimes those confrontations could get a bit heated. When Dean was roughly 15 years old he and his stepfather became intermingled in an ugly argument. That day, it was decided that it was time for Dean to venture out and find a job. Although I first started working at the age of 13, I thought it was too soon and a bit harsh for my husband to force Dean into work. We debated for a while but my husband felt it was the best thing to do. Always strong and with a rebellious spirit Dean jumped on his bike and headed out to find some work. They often say that great things come from tragic situations, well, this is a specific example.

A few hours after their fight Dean returned home and to my surprise he had some great news to share. Frantically, he told us that he was now the proud employee at one of the local cafés. I was shocked! Not only was I happy for my young man but I was completely surprised that he had pulled it off! Dean would soon be working in the kitchen of one of our favorite places to eat (who knew that a heated argument would open a door for so many future opportunities). He took to the restaurant business like a moth to a flame. Each day Dean found new opportunities to learn and better himself in the industry.

With each step that budding chef became more talented at his craft and he was quickly starting to design his life.

Dean has always loved to cook and finds the art extremely gratifying because it allows him to be creative. That zestful love for cooking led him to make a long trek from Florida to Chicago between his sophomore and junior years in high school. Big bro Nathan had since moved to Chicago so the two roomed together while Dean worked under a master chef (he was only 16 at the time so I naturally felt like I was being irresponsible for letting him go). However, in the long run the adventure and experience would be beneficial because it taught him about the harsh and sometimes unrelenting decisions we are faced with in life. Dean learned first-hand how difficult and demanding the "kitchen-life" was. Above all else, he was exposed to how crazy most head chefs can be. I mean that in the truest sense. As Dean worked his way up through the ranks, I've witnessed how demanding and grueling the restaurant industry is (not only working as a head chef but also as a sous-chef). That life is not only mentally taxing but it takes a toll on one's physical health.

That summer in Chicago was a huge test for Deano in regards to his culinary future. When he returned to Florida I could see in his eyes that he had passed with high marks. I knew how lucky he was to have such an opportunity to work in a hands-on environment at such a young age. After coming home to Florida he quickly nailed down a position in a country club. I often overheard his bosses express how impressed they were by his professional conduct and technical skill. My young chef didn't stop there and the very next summer he was off to Miami to work under another master chef. I could see that all of Dean's experiences were starting to melt and simmer together. A great chef was being cooked up right before my eyes.

As the name lends to itself, paradise is a magnificent home to many great restaurants. Over the span of about eight years Deano cooked up some special meals at a number of restaurants and wore many hats in the kitchen. When the workday was done it really didn't matter what hat he wore that day, his work always spoke for itself. Fortunately, he gained a great reputation that led many customers to flock back to his restaurants. Aside from the great technical skills of the culinary world he possesses, perhaps his best quality is how he works with others (even when it gets too hot in the kitchen). People truly enjoy working with Dean because he always makes sure to treat them like family. The great bond and love shared in a kitchen can be tasted in every dish that's served up. One of the biggest compliments a manager or boss can receive in the restaurant industry is when people say what a pleasure it is to work together. I guess you could say that in Dean's kitchen it is like paradise and not 'hell'! For me, it has always been important to instill the idea of acting as a mentor to anyone who needs the help.

Dean has since mentored many young people in the culinary arts. I've seen him step beyond the lines of the kitchen to help people, especially younger people dealing with trouble. It warms my heart to see that all of my sons have taken on the responsibility of being mentors in some capacity. Sometimes I'll find myself in one of Dean's kitchens being approached by his co-workers and staff – they greet me with the warmest hugs and always ask of how Deano is fairing.

Outside of the kitchen, there is one experience that Deano and I shared that stands out to this day; I still get goose bumps thinking about it. After a hard night's work in the kitchen Deano passed by my room and knocked on the door. He asked if we could talk for a bit and as he waltzed in I noticed a little picture in his hand. Dean handed it over to me and after a few seconds of examining the photo I couldn't make out what I was meant to be looking at. Then a light bulb sprung to life and I realized what he was trying to tell me – my little Deano and his girlfriend were going to have a baby!

Luckily I was lying down because my heart skipped a beat: I was stunned! Before I could ask him anything I noticed the look in his eyes and it instantly floored me. My boy's eyes welled up with glistening tears.

"Mom, I'm so excited about this. I want this baby with all of my heart," Dean said.

I didn't know what to say so I looked into his eyes and told him that I loved him and wanted the same. I made sure to let him know that I was excited to be a grandmother (I'm admitting here that I'm a grandmother).

They decided to name their baby Hope, and at an early age the little cutie has already shown similar traits of her father. Hope is a complete spark plug and full of fearless energy. We love our Hopie very much.

Dean's burning culinary passion has taken him out to California where he is now an executive chef at one of the largest restaurants in the nation. Deano continues to work hard and stays true to his code of treating his co-workers and staff like family. On a visit to the west coast I discovered that he is still a ball of non-stop energy and chooses to use his gifts to the best of his ability. What a true genuine article my boy is.

Now I feel it's appropriate to talk about my youngest son, W. Yes, His name is Mr. W; it's just one letter, an initial. When people aren't teasing him about his first "initial", he usually goes by his middle name, Blake. It suits him just fine.

When Blake was growing up he was the easiest to handle (or manage, it's not like he was a package). W was a beautiful tranquil baby and was blessed with a few physical attributes that his brother's were not. He had a few more rolls of baby-fat and although everyone tried, no one could find a single strand of hair on his precious baby head. My little Kojak was so adorable that I immediately fell in love with him and his perpetual smile.

Blake is certainly one of my most treasured blessings. I love admitting that because it always reminds me of how fortunate I am to have him. When I learned that I was pregnant with Blake, I had immediate doubts and struggled with the idea of giving birth to him. Whether or not to continue with the pregnancy was a dilemma that loomed heavily over my head like a swarm of confusing gray clouds: this is very difficult to speak of. I spent countless evenings praying to God so that he might help me find direction and to understand what the correct choice might be.

The main reason that I had doubts about giving birth was because my marriage to Blake's father was extremely explosive. When I learned of my pregnancy I had immediate doubts about things because of how incredibly turbulent my life was shaping up to be – especially in the relationship department. I was constantly questioning every tiny and minuscule detail of my life, which in turn just made everything more bewildering. The ultimate challenge was deciding whether or not to have a child with someone I didn't foresee a future with. I prayed long and hard for answers and after intense soul searching, I realized I wanted my child more than ever. My spirit told me that God wanted me to push forward and believe in his everlasting love and devotion. I decided to embrace the situation with faith and never looked back.

Blake and I have a connection that is, to put it simply, 'understood'. I kept him close to my side as he grew up and that has formed an impenetrable concrete bond between us. My youngest son grew up with me as his main parental figure, so I'm not only a mother to him but also a best friend. I've learned that 'W' has been blessed with natural intelligence and a perpetual inquisitiveness that compels him to face every challenge head on. In life, he always sticks to his guns (it's a trait that I hope he gained from his mother).

Although he is certainly very bright Blake has faced his share of obstacles. Over the years he's battled slight dyslexia (if you are unfamiliar with the term, it's when the letters get jumbled in someone's head as they read). To combat that hefty obstacle my Blake has found a way to use his intelligence to overcome that slight setback. How does he do it? Blake focuses on his love for music, art and literature to deal with challenges that might arise. With an absolute determination he has grown into a spectacular musician. With each pluck of the guitar strings and the distinct rhythm of his drum playing, he impresses to no end. There is no doubt in my mind that he was blessed with some of his grandfather's musical expertise. That natural talent helped 'W' teach him self how to play the saxophone, guitar and drums (he excels at the drums and after a solo, I must say, the girls are always begging for more).

After pushing through high school Blake began to construct his life's design. He and his cousin Geramie became very close friends and quickly formed a powerful musical duo. They were very driven and lusted after musical creation and innovation. The aspiring rock stars decided to blaze a path westward in hopes of creating as much music as possible. With my loving support and the support of our entire family, they fearlessly decided to set out on a cross-country adventure. But before they decided to do so, the dynamic duo and another band member went to a local recording studio to lay down some original material. That studio time and experience was so inspiring that it catapulted the boys to make that ultimate decision to head west. It was a time filled with excitement and endless possibilities and with Blake's older brothers already on the west coast, the move was meant to be. Before their rocket launch from Paradise the family had a huge blow out party. When any members of our wolf pack choose to leave for one avenue or another, we all made sure to send them off with great love and many heartfelt wishes.

Blake and Geramie were to drive separate cars and make a stop in Texas to visit family (who are musicians as well). The day finally came for my youngest to fly the coupe so I started to prepare myself for the inevitable heart-wrenching goodbyes. I tried to prepare myself as best I could— I certainly didn't want to break down and have another "first day of school" moment! I was coping with the idea of not only saying goodbye to my son but I had to adjust to being alone for the first time in decades.

Having raised my boys primarily on my own, I was accustomed to always having them around. That was the only life I knew and it was about to change forever. If you are a parent you know exactly what I'm talking about. Although I always attempted to be fearless, whether it's for my boys or for my-self, I realized I never had felt such a horrifying sensation. So with some spiritual assistance, it was best to put on my 'untouchable face' so to ease the sadness when Blake finally disappeared from the driveway.

After packing up his car the gravity of the time swept over me and I realized that my child was ready for his first real adventure without me. 'W' stood before me as a man and I froze. I couldn't move and just wanted to keep him all to myself. Blake slowly walked up to me and gave me a great big warm hug: we both held on for dear life. I thought it was going to take a pair of vice grips to separate us, but somehow we said our loving goodbyes. My rock star jumped into his car and slowly started down the driveway. As I watched, he stopped, popped his head out of the window and yelled, "I Love You Mom!" Then he was off.

As I watched him leave I collapsed in the driveway. It may sound dramatic but I couldn't help myself, I couldn't stop sobbing. I knew it was crucial that I 'let go', because it was the only way God could show Blake everything that he was meant to be. As I sat in the driveway with tears streaming down my face I looked up to heaven and asked God for one favor: I asked that he wrap my son within his powerful arms so that Blake could become the best person he could possibly be.

Over the years people often ask me if I have any bitter feelings towards the idea of marriage. They also ask if there are any negative thoughts or feelings harbored within towards my x-husbands. Sometimes I find myself talking with other divorcees and I can hear how much contempt they hold towards their x-partners. To answer the question of whether or not I harbor any anger I say this: my marriages presented me with challenging situations but it yielded my greatest joys – my three sons. My boys are the direct beautiful result of many of the great choices I've made in my life. If I were given the chance to do everything over I would make those same choices in a heartbeat. There might be a few tiny turns in the road that

I could have avoided to side step some chaos, but I would always choose to end up at the same destination. It's impossible to ask God, my creator, for anything else in life. I'm so grateful for his gifts and as I write I'm challenging my readers to reflect on your life. I challenge you to focus on the positive and to do away with the negative in its entirety. If you choose to rid yourself of the negative you will feel an indescribable liberation. Your daily life will begin to prosper and you will easily be able to mold your future life in such a divine and pleasant way. Life is a blessing if we all choose to embrace it with sincere and loving positivity.

This is one of the most challenging choices to make and perhaps the most important in life: to choose positivity over negativity. I have found such joy in my decisions to forgive and move on with the positive. If my sons learn anything from me as their mother, I hope with all of my being they choose positivity. I believe that if they do so, my boys will find the treasures of a lifetime.

My Three Sons: Dean, W Blake and Nathan

St. Bernice the Fearless

We have all dealt with turbulent times in our lives whether they have been matters of life, death or just surviving a rough time. Sometimes it's our support system that gets us through those tough times, other times it may have been just a stroke of luck. Mostly for me, I've always found strength and faith through one very powerful person, my mother. I often refer to her as St. Bernice the Fearless.

Growing up, my father embodied the essence of a strong patriarch in our household. To complement his strength my mom always carried herself like a proud and powerful matriarch. For my siblings and me, life was very well structure with my mother being the roots and sturdy base of our family tree. She adored her husband and doted on her children by instilling love and affection into our countless endeavors. That love extended beyond our immediate family and found its way into the lives of many of our friends and neighbors. My brothers and sisters talk fondly about the people who considered our mother as their own.

My mother devoted her life to God and all of his teachings; this gave her an unshakable fearlessness in every walk of life. She exuded courage and an undeniable loving spirit that transcends generations. One of her most powerful gifts was how she helped others with a magical spirit that ran through her. That spirit was a gift from God that brightly sparkled upon everything and graced anyone she touched.

My mother's love was manifested through a number of deep and devoted ACTS. She prayed to St. Anthony of Padua who is the patron saint of lost and stolen articles. Saint Anthony held a special place in my mother's heart; thankfully he looked upon her with special care because with seven kids came many *lost* things. There are too many times to count when she asked for help to find a treasure that had gone missing; but that is exactly what Mom did and her prayers were always answered.

Above all else, my mother was soulfully connected to The Blessed Mother Mary. Bernice spoke many times to me about how she thought about Mother Mary having to watch others crucify her son all the while continuing to love and have faith in God. My mother had the greatest amount of love and respect for the Virgin Mary because of her undying dedication and faith in her son and God. That common spirit that they had for God and their children was a bond that would never be broken.

I believe it was her lifelong faith that helped St. Bernice deal with everything in life, especially my father's passing. Admittedly, my family and I didn't think she would fare well in the months following dad's death; but to everyone's surprise she found the strength and rose to the challenge. Mom didn't let her sorrows bring her down and appeared so unfazed that my family was worried that she was simply suppressing her grief. After years of such an intense and close connection with her husband we all thought it impossible for her to heal so quickly. Even if she found herself in pain or in need of assistance, mom never thought of placing a burden on anyone. We all realized that she was an incredibly strong person, but we also knew that times were changing and we would have to face reality sooner or later – the reality that our mother would be making was her own transition.

Shortly after my father's passing, mom and I often engaged in deep and heartfelt conversations about life and death: we never held anything back. One idea we enjoyed playing with was creating a way for us to communicate after mom moved on to the next life. We both thought about it often but weren't able to solidify a plan (cosmic scientists we weren't). However, we knew that God would show us the way in his own good time and we were sure to ready ourselves for when that time came.

Life is filled with blessings whether they are grand or small in scale. My family was extremely fortunate that our mother was able to stay active and independent as she moved into her later years. My sister Bernadette and her husband Butch (bless their hearts) were able to care for mom in their home where they shared many precious times. One of their most favorite past-times was taking peaceful walks through my sister's quiet neighborhood. As a whole, our family knew how blessed we were to share those moments. Even when she wasn't feeling up to it, mom always found a way to share her time with us.

St. Bernice's vibrant love washed over everyone she encountered. Aside from her family she also made sure to shower her friends with affection. One good friend of mine that she took a special shine to was my friend Patrick. Mom had a profound respect for him because of the great dedication he had for his work and country. Although my mother didn't agree with some of Patrick's choices in regards to his relationships, she always held a special place for him in her heart. One of her most challenging times came when I told her just how much I cared for Patrick. I believe that my mom felt I was in danger of heading down a turbulent road, so she couldn't give her full support: it was unchartered water for us. For my mother and I to disagree on anything was frighteningly foreign; at times I felt like I was being strongly judged for the decisions I was making. Yes, it all hurt me deeply but I kept silent and never complained nor questioned anything. As my relationship with Patrick grew my mom's doubts began to turn into anxiety. I was at a loss for words every time the subject would come up. The complex relationship that I had developed with Patrick came out into the open and my family couldn't help but let me know that it was affecting our mother.

My family sensed her disapproval but we could all feel that she was dealing with other personal issues, something distant and foreign. She started to display a sort of restlessness that none of us knew how to handle. My brother Gary suggested that mom talk to me about her concerns, which thankfully she did. I can now say I was happy she decided to confront me, but at the time I felt completely devastated. We shared a long conversation discussing her views of how I was living my life. After that intense mother-to-daughter talk, I remember leaving the house feeling down and extremely ashamed (all in all, it wasn't a good night).

Shortly after I took a vacation with my boys for Blake's 21st birthday. I was consumed with sadness and some guilt as to how I was affecting my mom; but just like always, I knew that standing strong in the midst of despair was the only way to go. I told myself that my mother wasn't trying to diminish my choices but that she was only trying to open my eyes to what I deserved in life. During that time in Vegas, I prepared myself to resolve my issues concerning Patrick with my mother when I returned home.

Well, as they say: what happens in Vegas stays in Vegas. That maxim held true because when I got back to paradise all I could do was make a b-line for bed. I was another victim of the playground in the desert (a willing victim). I woke the next morning and immediately called my sister to learn how mom was doing. Bernadette eased my tensions by letting me know that mom was fine although dealing with some nausea. My sister asked if I wanted to speak to her and when I heard my mom's voice, I sensed a distance between us. I didn't think the tension was because of the conversation we had before I left for Vegas – it was something that she was dealing with that she obviously didn't want to discuss over the phone. I let Bernadette know that I wanted some alone time with our mother that evening.

That night I arrived just as Bernadette was leaving the house and as I entered I looked lovingly upon my mother as she sat relaxed in her favorite chair. After spending some time with her I noticed she wasn't paying much attention to the television but was staring aimlessly out into the distance. I placed a soft kiss upon her forehead and starting telling some colorful Vegas stories in order to lighten her spirit. I went on and on about the trip and tried to be as entertaining as possible. My efforts were futile. My mother continued to stare into a type of nothingness that was puzzling me. Convinced that she didn't want to hear about the trip, I knew it was time to discuss my relationship with Patrick. I really wasn't sure if I was ready for that conversation. A short time passed and my need to get things out into the open almost turned into a radical desperation. The need welled up inside of me so I found my inner-strength, stood up, and walked over to her. Sitting on the floor in front of her, I took her soft and delicate hand into mine and said, "Mom. What is going on with you?"

Her reaction or lack thereof startled me. To my surprise she didn't even look my way and just stared into her distant outer world. I decided to give it another go.

I asked, "Mom, are you alright?"

"I don't want to talk about it," she quickly rebutted.

The first thought that sprung into my mind was that she was extremely upset with me. I was heartbroken.

"Why don't you want to talk mom? We always talk about everything," I pleaded. "Remember... You and I are best friends who can talk about anything."

With her eyes starting to swell with tears, she said, "I am done."

I was confused and felt like I was standing on the outside looking in.

"Done? What do you mean you're done?" I pleaded.

She answered, "I mean I can't go north this summer with Bernadette. I want to stay here."

Mom always loved going north to visit family and friends for the summer so I couldn't understand what the issue was. Was it physical? Was there something emotionally troubling her that she was hiding?

Then, with a hallowing tone, she told me, "Because I am ready to go."

I asked what she meant by that and in my heart, I needed and wanted an instant explanation. As I asked her to tell me a wave of panic washed over me. It was the feeling I got when I knew something life changing was about to happen. After a long pause she softly explained what she was feeling.

"I am ready to be with your dad and God," she said with a stern conviction.

"Mom, I don't think you have the choice to do that. I think God makes the ultimate decision of when it's your time to join him," I said.

In an instant – just after saying that, I knew I was wrong. It hit me: I realized that my mother gave her entire life over to God and her absolute faith to all of his teachings. I reiterate that she was perpetually fearless because of her unrelenting trust in God. In return, God would always be there for her. I did my best to accept and begin to cope with St. Bernice's life altering plans.

"Mom, I hear you. I promise to do everything I can to make whatever you want happen," I said to calm her in any way possible. She hugged me and told me that she loved me. I sat in a daze and held her hand.

A little while later Butch came into the house and we instantly caught each other's eyes (there was the feeling something was gravely wrong). He motioned for me to follow him into the kitchen where, with welling eyes, he questioned, "She's giving up, isn't she?" I lightly nodded yes – no words were needed.

The panic that had been brewing beneath my surface was starting to boil over. I asked myself, 'Why did she choose to tell me?' How would I break the news to Bernadette and the rest of my family? The most profound question that hit me was, 'What in heaven's name do we do now?' As the hundreds of questions flooded my mind I started to hyperventilate. Internally, I wondered how everyone would react to the news or even if they would grasp the finality of it all. I didn't have time to come up with any secure answers because just then in walked Bernadette. I briefly tried some small talk by asking how everything was; that approach was useless. I couldn't get my mom's confession out of my head and I needed to talk to my sister.

"I have to go, can you come on out to the car with me?" I asked her.

As she gazed aimlessly, I kissed my mom gently on the forehead and let her know I would talk to her the following day. Bernadette and I walked to my car and as I tried to explain everything, I felt she would be able to see the actual pain in my words. Simply and directly to the point I told my sister that our mother was ready to be with dad and God. Bernadette's initial reaction was she believed our mom wasn't ready to go; that mom had been a bit lethargic lately but that didn't warrant her being anywhere near ready to pass on. My family always knew that mom never wanted to pose a burden on anyone and that was the reason she remained somewhat quiet. Bernadette and I decided to regroup the following day in order to work out a plan. It was best to beseech the help of my brother Gary and sister Carol (most importantly, I needed God). As I drove home that night I felt completely numb and humbled by the power of life.

We set a meeting for the next day and I honestly didn't know what we would say to each other. How does a loving family talk about their mother's imminent passing? First we talked about the past few weeks concerning our interactions with her and we all agreed that mom had become intensely anxious. It was as if she wanted to get her life's affairs in order. Many questions started to arise at that point, one major subject was: What would happen in the coming months? Bernadette was supposed to travel with mom back to Michigan in the next few weeks and spend the summer there. We couldn't figure out if that was a good idea and how it would eventually affect the 'big picture'. I decided to speak up.

"I don't think mom's passing will take a long time. I think we all need to recognize that," I mustered up the courage to say.

Then, thankfully, my sister and her husband relieved some of the tension by telling us they decided not to go to Michigan for the summer and stay back with mom.

We all breathed a sigh of relief after they broke the news because Bernadette and Butch were my mom's primary caregivers for many years. After some debate as to what the best course of action would be, we all knew there was only one suitable decision. My family had to face the heartbreaking task of letting our beloved mother know that we supported any choice she would make (whether or not we wanted to commit her to the next life). Bernadette did her best to ease the anxiety by letting us know she would take mom for a thorough medical check-up. After sorting out those new and tumultuous decisions, my brothers, sisters and I embraced each other in an enormous hug. In that hug we sealed our resolve to support our mother's choice to stay in paradise and not return to Michigan. We chose to embrace life's inevitable mysteries no matter what God had in store for us.

Over the next few days Bernadette and I shared with mom that we all understood and accepted her wishes with all of our love. However, as is common with many adults graduating into their senior years, my mom had fears we would place her into a nursing home. This was the farthest thing from our minds and we actually teased her about the idea. We laughed it off and assured her that we could never put her in someone else's care. To our surprise she was extremely chipper and coherent, more than she had been in months. That was certainly a plus.

The strength and support of family was what carried everyone through that heart wrenching time. Bernadette was a veracious trooper who acted as the primary care giver, taking mom back and forth to her doctor's appointments. During the doctor's appointment after our family meeting Bernadette was told mom was doing very well and that some test results would lend more information. That weekend went smoothly in regards to mom's physical health, but Bernadette and Butch noticed some peculiar behavior. She was becoming more distant and not eating well. I also noticed the change and felt that my mother was starting to drift out to sea all by her lonesome: a great uneasiness crept into my heart. That uncertainty manifested itself when I received an alarming call from Bernadette that Monday morning.

She said, "Listen, Carol and I are on our way to the hospital. We had to call an ambulance to pick mom up at the house."

With a bewildered tone I asked, "It's starting, isn't it?"

"I don't know but she's been bad all night. The doctor called to let us know that her tests showed there will be some challenges ahead and it would be in our best interest to take her to the hospital for observation," she explained.

At that moment I knew: This was it. It was time to face my mother's condition head-on. After summoning some strength I made my way to the hospital's E.R. My sisters and I held hands vigilantly while we waited. That was a gut wrenching time because the hospital allowed only one visitor in the E.R. at a time.

While we waited I realized it was only six days since our mother first told us she was ready to unite with dad and God. I couldn't help but dwell on the idea that I would have to support my mother's difficult choice. How could we do it? My family was blessed when a hospital staff member allowed all of us back into the E.R. to see her. Mom was in a medicated hazy daze and extremely upset that she was subjected to intravenous feeding. She was against being kept alive through artificial means and didn't want anything to interrupt her natural transition to the next life. At that time it was necessary to present the legal documents so that the physicians could legally cease all preventative health care. In doing so, we all hoped that she could obtain the blissful sleep that she longed for.

Carol returned with the documents after Bernadette and I allowed doctors to take x-rays of mom's chest (we were still hoping they could find a reason for her quick decline). Needless to say mom wasn't thrilled with us because she detested any medical assistance. After listening to her laments, Bernadette and I took a great (but hesitant) leap of faith by telling the hospital to stop all of the tests they were doing and any that were planned. Things were getting more serious and time was becoming more crucial. The smart voice in my head told me to contact everyone in my family as quickly as possible: I knew the time was coming. After some routine legal issues were covered in regards to my mother's wishes to stop medical treatment, the hospital agreed to respect her and left things to fate. I began to call each of my brothers one by one, not knowing and very afraid of how they were going to react.

The terrific and solid bond of my family never ceases to fail me when faced with a crisis. My siblings held strong and accepted the decision to let mom find her way into God's arms the way she wanted to. My family requested that I keep them posted as to every new development so I promised to do so as best I could. We were on board and ready for an earth shattering experience. At that time I realized that it was our spiritual obligation to follow a certain plan; not our chosen plan, but the plan that God would lay out before us.

My mother's declining health wasn't the result of an accident or a disease: it was a natural occurrence. That fact made coping with her illness extremely painful. I had to find acceptance in the difficult decision for her to make her final transition. Every child who has ever had a deep loving connection with their mother knows there isn't an easy way to come to grips with losing her. Time passed and I continually questioned the right course of action to take. I could not be selfish, that wasn't the way we dealt with things in our family. My mother's children held steady to her wishes, knowing that God would show us the way.

After her stay in the emergency room doctors moved her to a comfortable hospital room. Standing around mom's bed my siblings and I looked at each other and knew it was just a matter of waiting patiently for God to intervene. At the time, mom was being administered pain medication to alleviate some back pain she was experiencing (with her permission of course). I found it curious that although she was heavily medicated and sometimes drifted off to distant places, other times mom seemed to be quite lucid and could hold lengthy conversations. I adored our talks and was fascinated by the things she said.

My mother would say to us, "It's not what you think Mary. You go from here to there and then you start all over again. It's in reverse."

When she said those profound things everyone just assumed the drugs were starting to kick in. Then, when we would ask what she meant she was extremely hard to understand and reach. She was adrift and in her own world of thought. Her condition became more serious so we decided it was time to call on a priest to bless my mother with Final Absolution. Throughout the Catholic religion it is understood that Final Absolution is among the last steps one takes before leaving this earth; my family was completely aware of the intense implications. God must have been listening to us because shortly after making the decision, we turned a hospital corner and saw a chaplain who was a long time friend of the family.

"Hi! How are you doing?" the chaplain asked.

Astonished, Bernadette and I just looked at each other. The chaplain was doing his daily rounds at the hospital when he happened upon us in our greatest time of need. We quickly informed him of mom's situation in hopes that he could lend his assistance. Graciously, he gave his blessing and said that he would notify the church so that they could send a priest.

The day was turning into night, so I told my sisters that it was all right for them to head home. I would stay with mom and hold her hand with love. Feeling unprepared for what might happen I had to force my nerve-racked emotions down into the pit of my stomach. After doing so a peaceful sleep came over me as I nuzzled to my mother. A couple hours later I was awoke by my mom's voice: she was calling out to me, "Mary, are you there?"

I said softly, "Yes mom, I'm right here."

She asked, "Can you please ask the nurse to bring a little pain medication? I'm in so much pain."

I could see how uncomfortable she was so I scrambled to find some help. The first available nurse was a sweetheart who told me she would tend to my mother as soon as possible. She administered some pain medication that sent my mom off into a silky sleep. I used that time to make some important phone calls and while I got in touch with the outside world I received a heartwarming call from Patrick. He wanted to know how my mom was doing and it absolutely meant the world to me. I let him know how things were going, that conversation made me realize how fortunate I was to have such a great friend to lean on.

During that night my mom sailed in and out of a blissful sleep. During her most lucid times she gazed into the distance and continually talked about a 'cycle' of life.

She tried to explain, "It's not what you think. You're here and then you're there. It's in reverse and you start at the beginning. There is no end. We just go back to the beginning. It's in reverse."

When she was more lucid I would lay my head next to her as we talked softly. My mother would tell me wonderful things about her children, grandchildren and even great grandchildren. We discussed how much she loved her parents and siblings; she was one of 15 children. Of course she spoke of my father and his family as well. She would stroke my hair to calm my fears. We talked about everything, well, what seemed like everything. My mother and I connected on a beautiful spiritual level. However, during one of our conversations I was shocked to hear my mother say...

"Mary, will you forgive me?" mom asked me.

I desperately asked, "What on earth are you asking me to forgive you for?"

She said, "I judged you when I had no right to. I judged you for the way you were handling your relationship with Patrick. I judged both of you and I had no right to. I've stood by and watched you live without having someone who deserves you by your side. You've spent most of your adult life raising your family on your own and I always wanted more for you. I only wanted for you what I always had with your father. No one deserves to have someone by his or her side more than you. I could only watch as you loved Patrick very deeply although he chose not to fully commit to you."

I was frozen.

She said, "I realize what an incredible person you are and that it would take a very strong person to stand by your side. You ask for nothing and never place your needs ahead of anyone else. That quality you have is truly the epitome of unconditional love. Who am I to say what's right for you? The truth is… I admire you so much. You have done so many things for others, mainly for your family. Most importantly, you've been fearless and haven't asked for anything in return."

My heart sank as a powerful and leveling feeling covered my soul.

She asked again, "Will you please forgive me? Forgive me for fearing for you. I now know that it's not my place to do so. I know you are right with God and I'm proud of the person you are. Also, please tell Patrick that I love him."

The tears streamed down my cheeks. I remember thinking that perhaps the most important thing I didn't want to happen before mom passed was for her to hold any judgment against me: I just wouldn't be able to bear it. At that point it was though God gave me the gift of my mom asking me to forgive her. She realized that I was just doing what she had taught me and that was to love unconditionally no matter how much it hurt. *She taught me to love through the hurt and forgive through the pain.* There was no way I was leaving my mother's side (horses couldn't drag me away and sleep deprivation was no match). I was determined to keep strong and push through the pain in order to share every last waking minute with my mother.

The following day Bernadette, Carol and I spent the day with mom. Although she was drifting in and out of consciousness we found it impossible to leave her for a second without her calling out to us. I was amazed at how heightened her sense of hearing had become; she could actually hear us having a conversation from down the hall. In my life, as I have matured and gained wisdom, I've learned more about how human physiology tends to change in fascinating ways. My mother always knew who was in the room... even if she was sleeping.

After a hospice nurse spent some time evaluating mom's condition, we were told it wasn't time to move her just yet. The nurse felt it would be best to either take mom to a nursing facility or back home to be with us: we weren't onboard with either option. Carol, Bernadette and I retreated to the hospital cafeteria to analyze the situation. After some debate we went back to mom's room and were immediately faced with another challenge. Our mother was sitting up in bed enjoying her breakfast as if it was the first meal she's ever had! With wide eyes and a bright spirit she ranted about how delicious the hot coffee and eggs were. Without question, we were astounded. Just an hour before it appeared she was knocking on heaven's door. Although she had directives not to eat or drink, she ignored everything and did as she pleased. It was all very confusing. My sisters and I started to think that perhaps mom had a change of heart and decided to push on with life. Seeing her in such a jovial mood made it all the more painful to go along with her wishes. How could we agree with her decision to pass on when she seemed to be going in a different direction?

A little later that day Father Ed entered the room to perform Final Absolution (making the situation even more perplexed). As a family we felt it was the right choice to make and allow the kindhearted priest to bless our mother. My family had many religious ties with Father Ed because we were all from Michigan; that made everything more comfortable. Personable, warm, and inspiring are all great words to describe our friend Father Ed. As a group we held hands and surrounded our mother for prayer. We said the 'Our father', the prayers for her final absolution and then gave mom communion. The prayers and love floating throughout the room were incredible, we all felt connected and at peace.

It was in that moment that we looked down on our mother's tranquil face. With a quick jerk-like motion, she dropped her head to her chest and expected to be taken by God immediately. We all looked at each other and couldn't conjure up words.

I thought, "Does mom actually think that God is going to take her this very moment? Did she think that Final Absolution was the immediate gateway to heaven?"

Her kids and even father Ed were baffled. It occurred to me that my mother's faith was so strong that she believed God would take her that instant. When a few moments passed she opened her eyes and grabbed Carol's hand.

Mom asked, "Why are you still here?"

It was obvious she realized that death hadn't come to greet her as she expected. When mom opened her eyes, Carol was still standing right there beside her. As we slowly realized what had happened there was only one thing to do: We burst out laughing! It was all purely heartfelt so the laughter just came naturally.

Laughter and playfulness have been the cornerstones of the prolonged happiness in my family. No matter what the scenario, we always search for the lighter side of life. I guess we now also look at the lighter side of death. Soon thereafter, father Ed said his goodbyes and asked to be informed about mom's condition because he wanted to personally perform the services when the time called. The next hours were perplexing in that we weren't sure what was in store, Final Absolution was meant to be one of the last steps in a person's life on earth. We didn't know what direction to take so we went with our hearts. My brothers, sisters and I put our faith in the idea that God and mom would show us the way. I stayed until the sun rose again the next morning, all while holding hands with her. That night was filled with her drifting in and out of sleep and repeating what she had said earlier, "It's not what you think. You go from here to there and then you start all over again. It's in reverse."

I tried to grasp the concept of what she was saying but I couldn't wrap my head around the idea. Most importantly, I remember thinking that I ultimately didn't want my mother to suffer in any way towards the end of her life here on earth. I continually beseeched God to spare my mother any discomfort.

I felt that God had his arms around me during those moments, I could almost hear him saying, "Trust me, I will not fail you". I took a deep breath, asked for forgiveness and thanked God for promising to spare her. I looked down to see that Patrick was ringing me on my phone. I went to the hallway to talk with him for a bit and then returned and laid my head upon mom's chest.

As she woke she gently stroked my hair and asked, "Mary, how can I go if you are still here?"

Then it was time to stand strong and I said, "I don't know mom, but I'm not going anywhere. God and you will have to figure it out with me sitting right here."

She agreed and then asked if I would sing to her; one of mom's favorite songs was 'You Are So Beautiful' written by Billy Preston and sung by Joe Cocker. Before I could start to sing she drifted off into a quiet slumber, so I whispered in her ear that I would sing before she left me.

I spent yet another night drifting in and out of sleep next to mom's bedside. My sister Carol arrived at the hospital the next day so that allowed me some time to head home. I returned to the hospital with hopes of being able to speak with my sisters about some important and impending decisions. We decided to have another hospice nurse review our mother's condition in hopes of getting the best care necessary. With God watching over, the hospice nurse just happened to be on our floor and she agreed to evaluate our mother's condition. The nurse let us know that it was best to send mom home with a 24 hour nursing monitor in order to gauge her health more thoroughly. Although I remember feeling relieved that my mom would have home nursing care, my heart sank and was consumed with the reality that she was actually starting her life's transition. *It was happening.*

Within a few hours Bernadette and Ron, my brother-in-law, transformed my sister's living room into a private sanctuary (the nurse set up the necessary medical equipment). From that experience I can truly say how special and majestic hospice care professionals are. We got so many visits from all sorts of people during mom's stay at my sister's; family and friends wanted to stop by and share some special time with her. Among those caring visitors were two of my great friends, Anna and Jeannie. They both loved and cared for my mom as if she was their own. Those times are cherished because when mom woke up and talked with everyone, she would always light up the room. By constantly telling everyone how much she loved them mom always made everyone feel comfortable in her powerful embrace. It was the Thursday before Easter and I remember a large number of people stopping by the house. During the day my mom actually shocked me by saying, "You know that I won't be here for Easter, don't you?"

"All right mom," was all I could say. I understood.

I hoped she wouldn't pass on Holy Thursday, Good Friday or Easter Sunday so that she could spend those holy days with family. With the help from those amazing nurses my family was able to sleep soundly that night, I in my own bed. The following morning I headed to Bernadette's and quickly asked everyone about mom's condition as I quietly prayed to God. Nurses explained that her breathing had become irregular and she had fallen unconscious during the night. Shortly thereafter we received a call from the hospice care center saying they had a bed and were ready to receive her. Things were beginning to move rapidly.

I remember fearing that mom would pass away on the trip to the hospice center. My heart was fluttering and surprisingly, just the opposite happened. She began to find some hidden strength and I knew that my mother was a fighter who wanted to keep fighting the good fight.

I thought to myself, "Thank God".

When we arrived at the hospice center mom seemed to have a newfound energy. Just after the nurses nestled her into a new room, once again, visitors started to pour in.

My family and I made sure to surround her with vibrant life and love no matter what.

St. Bernice's love had reached far and wide. The impact she usually made was powerful and often made indelible impressions. Patrick called me again that afternoon to check in on the situation. He wanted me to know that he told the Army he needed to take some time off for personal matters. Fortunately, he was able to get away. While Patrick told me the news I realized that he was actually sticking to his promise and doing everything he could to be by my side. It meant so much to me because I knew that my mother wanted to know that Patrick was there. Also, he needed to be able to say goodbye to mom in his own way. It was comforting to know the three of us would have an opportunity to be together one last time. Although I sensed that mom wanted something a bit different for me, she would be able to see that what I had with Patrick truly made me happy. Not only did we love each other but also, our friendship will always stand true.

My parents had roughly 50 grand children and great grandchildren. Even with so many names and faces to remember I knew mom would find the strength to say goodbye to all of us. Countless nieces and nephews visited hospice to pay their respects and we all found a way to have fun and celebrate. A major family tradition was finding the joy and lighter side of life in the face of human struggle (that was one of my parent's most powerful examples). One key player in creating some family fun is my nephew George who is a very talented trumpet player. He came to visit mom and to make sure he played for her one more time. I know my mother took great joy in listening to the music and voices that lovingly swirled around her room. We were blessed to have that time in order to pay proper tribute to St. Bernice the Fearless.

After countless heartfelt prayers most of my family started for home. Suddenly, there he was: Patrick. As my knight in shining armor approached I couldn't wait to be wrapped in his warm embrace. A renewed sense of strength welled up inside of me because I instantly knew he would be there to stand by my side. I was also comforted by the idea that he would be able to say goodbye to mom in a way he wanted. I thanked God immediately as I usually did as a daily routine.

The sun rose with a spectacular brightness early the next morning. Patrick and I went to the hospice and learned that mom's breathing had held strong through the night. I was relieved to know that she wasn't suffering and I made sure to spend that marvelous day treasuring every moment that I could. During the day Patrick and I found a warm patio just outside of mom's room. There under a soft peaceful light I had the chance to thank Patrick for keeping his promise to be by my side. In return and with respect, he thanked me for allowing him to say goodbye to my mom. Patrick really did love her very much.

We went back into the room and my pilot returned to mom's bedside as I used the restroom. When I came out a blitzed look was painted on his face: I instantly knew something was wrong.

He said, "I kissed her forehead, she feels clammy and cold. I also noticed that her breathing is really labored."

I placed my hands under the blanket to check her body; she felt frighteningly cold. I noticed a sort of 'modeling' taking shape over her body (I wondered if it was normal for people nearing death). After I noticed the difference of how she felt, I panicked because Patrick and I were the only people in the room. I quickly ran to the lobby to find some help after realizing that if my mother's time was near I wanted my family to be there. I asked a nurse to check on mom and as I waited for an assessment, I was instantly relieved to see my sister Carol and her husband enter the room. We all needed courage and loving support so when my sister peered into my eyes, she could see the concern and trepidation deep within my soul. My concern was justified when the nurse told me it would be best to notify my family that *the time* was approaching. Therefore, we felt it would be appropriate to gather around our St. Bernice in love to pray the 'Hail Mary'.

My family was raised in the Catholic faith so saying that special prayer meant the world to my mom mainly because of the special relationship she held with the blessed Mother. With voices on high we prayed so that God may spare my mother any pain as she made her journey to the next life. Panic is usually something I don't usually succumb to, but right after our prayer I broke down and started to hyperventilate. My entire world was rapidly changing and my mind didn't want to deal with the severity of it. I did my best to calm down and focus on the task at hand: making my mom as comfortable as possible. All I could do was sit down, relax and force myself to breathe.

The most important thing was that I needed to be strong and show my mom that faith would see us through to a peaceful end. The first order of business was to alert my family of how critical her condition was so I frantically began to call everyone. I feared that I wouldn't be able to get everyone to the hospital in time, and for that I wouldn't have been able to forgive myself. After some time passed I again checked with the nurse.

In a soft tone she said, "This must be the way God wants it to be. There's a reason you two girls are here, the oldest and the youngest."

After hearing that comment from the nurse a moment of clarity washed over my spirit. I realized my mother knew her family was going to be alright in the future but there were just a few concerns about Carol and I that she was dealing with. With enormous tears streaming about the room, we all continued to pray. Carol and Ron stood on one side of the bed while Patrick and I were on the other; we held hands over our mother's fragile body. During prayer we placed our hands on her chest to let mom know we were with her. At that moment I remembered the promise I made to her in the hospital: I promised to sing for her one last time before she left us all. She wanted me to sing the song 'You Are So Beautiful'. I didn't know if I could do it... I was trembling.

I asked my sister, "How can I do this? I promised to sing before she left."

Carol simply asked, "Can you do it? If you can, we're here for you."

I reached down to find strength and said, "Yes. I can."

I began to sing....

You are so beautiful to me.

You are so beautiful to me.

Can't you see?

You're everything we hoped for and once more.

You are everything we need.

You are so beautiful to me.

You are so beautiful to me.

You are so beautiful to me, can't you see?

You're like guiding light shining in the night.

You are heaven to me.

You are so beautiful.

You are so beautiful.

You are so beautiful to me.

I finished singing and tried to control myself, I began to cry. As I wept I just couldn't stop the river of tears. I looked down to say goodbye to my mother and I couldn't believe my eyes. There it was, a beautiful single tear running down her soft cheek. Oh my God, she heard me sing! I feel God let her cry so I would know she heard me.

With our hands tightly bonded over her chest, mom said good-bye to us with one last breath: and then she was gone. I was devastated and let out a cry. I buried my head in Patrick's chest. The nurse motioned to us that her time had come.

We walked out of her room completely drained. Just then my brother in-law Butch arrived with my nephews. They entered the room to say their goodbyes to their grandmother. Although my mind was swimming with sadness we realized that Bernadette wasn't there at the time mom passed (she had just briefly stepped away). Carol and I began to worry about how we would break the news to her. Butch walked into the hall and noticed Bernadette walking towards us. All he could say was, "She's gone." Bernadette just collapsed. My heart sank and I felt her pain knowing that she would have given anything to be by our mother's side one last time before she passed. I hurriedly consoled Bernadette and put her at ease by telling her that mom treasured all the love and care she had given her over the years. I made it as clear as possible to my sister that mom was at peace with her not being there.

The entire experience was painstaking and tested my spiritual beliefs in ways that I had never felt. My family and I still deal with the passing of our beloved St. Bernice to this day with undeniable faith and love.

After my grieving and painful times, I now realize how incredible everything was. I reflect on the time leading up to her death and now understand that mom was making her transition peaceful not only for herself, but for her family as well. She continually led us to believe that her time was near and that we should all trust in the plan that God and her were putting into action. That plan blessed my family with nearly two weeks of love with our mother that still connects us to God forever. Mom was also blessed to have the opportunity of asking for my forgiveness for judging my relationship with Patrick. She could ultimately comprehend what my relationship was truly about. Instead of her leaving this life with any doubts, my mother was at peace with the choices and

designs that had been made by her ever-loving family.

An Unexpected Gift from God

Losing my mother was an extremely painful experience but it was the love and strength of family that saw everyone through. At the time I decided the best and healthiest course of action was to keep myself busy by getting the important things in life done. I engulfed myself in every detail of my mother's wake so that things would be just perfect. As I coordinated her wake I realized it was like trying to contain a mild tornado; my phone never stopped ringing. My voicemail was bubbling over with messages from family and friends who wanted to pay their last respects (so many, that I couldn't receive any more messages!).

One day I decided that I needed to sift through the messages and delete any that I could. Suddenly, there it was: I heard my mother's angelic voice sing out to me. For anyone who has longed to hear the voice of their loved ones that have gone, you know the joy that hearing their voice can bring. Before she passed away my mother and I actually talked about how we could communicate after she passed to the next life. It's certainly an intrinsic human emotion that children long to be close with their parents even after death. Ultimately, we believed that our strong spiritual faith and God's loving glow would assist us. The voice message was mom's way of saying hello from her new life, wherever that might have been. Her wonderful voice, laced with love and consumed by protectiveness, resonated through my spirit. I sensed the love in her voice as it wrapped my heart in warmth and comfort.

After I listened to her message I realized that it was older and one that I must have skipped over. I checked the date and realized that she must have called me during my flight to Vegas for Blake's 21st birthday. How could I have missed it? I realized mom sent the message a few days after she and I had a passionate discussion about my relationship with Patrick. I remember feeling upset about the situation and it was clear she felt the same way (mom called just to check in and to make sure I was alright and to tell me that she loved me).

Mom ended her message by saying, "I love you."

I hold that message tightly to my heart. It is God's unexpected gift to me and I listen to it often. It gives me special comfort in the middle of some lonely nights. When I hear her ask me to call her back I say out loud, "Mom, I'm calling and I love you very much".

I play that message for my family when the time calls for it. My mother's voice, warm and gentle, always brings a smile to everyone's face.

Loving Message

How do you create a celebration for a Saint? My heart told me it wasn't just my family who wanted to have a magical wake for mom, but God was telling me that it needed to be very special as well. My family became even closer and bonded during the planning process. We prayed and did everything together; walking alongside each other just as we had done when we first learned mom wanted to be with dad and God.

Preparing for the wake was a monumental task. As a family we selected a number of songs and prayers that we knew mom would adore. One of the last things to choose was a fitting casket for our mother's eternal rest. The funeral director showed us to the selection room, but before entering we embraced in a huge glowing hug that melted my heart. When we entered the showroom a lovely silver-blue casket mesmerized us. It was simply beautiful. The color blue always surrounded my mom with beauty and peace, so after some discussion, we took God's lead and chose it with confidence.

My family had some unique requests in regards to my mother's wake and funeral arrangements. I thank the Catholic Church for granting our wishes during that time; they gave us a great amount of leeway when adding to the ceremony. My brother Gary sang the 'Our Father' and his daughter Gina sang the 'Ave Maria'. I felt it was God's way of saying, "Trust in me, I will make the celebration one to be remembered."

The funeral was magnificent and abuzz with people shedding tears of love. The sermons were powerful and accompanied with incredible music. My boys arranged their busy schedules so they could attend their grandmother's funeral. Having all three of my sons by my side was a true blessing; I needed every ounce of their love and support. My mother was also surrounded by many of her grandchildren and great grandchildren. Some made long treks from distant states to be in Florida to show their love and to pay their respects. I was dazzled when Patrick arrived dressed in his Army uniform to honor our mother. He stood by my side and held my hand, gently giving me a great feeling of strength.

God's plans were in effect. The next part of our spiritual journey was to make our way to the gravesite. Family and friends gathered under a shelter constructed directly over where my mom would rest eternally next to her beloved Henry. Everyone was there and ready to say goodbye. During the celebration my nephew George brought out his trumpet to serenade his grandmother and family with one last beautiful song. He played the song, "Somewhere over the Rainbow." As George played I can remember thinking that it all must have been a dream.

At ceremony's end, my mother's seven children approached her casket together with a signature yellow rose in hand. As a family unit we placed the roses one by one on top of her beautiful silvery-blue casket. We gazed lovingly upon her with soft smiles, placed our hands on her casket and then we each kissed her goodbye one last time.

I had to compose myself after the ceremony because I knew it was important to stay strong; not only for myself but also for the entire family. The next part of God's plan was for everyone to go to a quaint church where Gary is the musical director (that's when things came alive with music and so much needed fun). Everyone chose his or her own special tribute to mom. In particular, Gary was always called upon to provide the music at family gathering. Weddings, parties, holidays and funerals, Gary could tackle the biggest events and he never refused. At the end of our unbelievable service, the seven of us stood side-by-side and started to sing the song: "When You Walk Through a Storm". While we sang, I felt as though we were kids again singing for our incredible mother and father.

That entire experience was utterly powerful. Although my family has had many great celebrations that meant so much, I can say that my mother's final celebratory goodbye was exceedingly special. That time was and will always be cherished.

I want to recite a prayer that my mother gave to me before she passed on.

It read: my gift to each of you is that we have shared touching moments in our lives that are to be cherished – moments that are captured and framed for eternity. Use these memories to remind you of how much I love you all. I want you to always remember how grateful I am to have had God, Henry, my children and their families in my life.

Lovingly Yours,

Bernice

Justin Time

After my mother passed away I wanted to hide from life so I escaped to my bedroom, again, in order to cope. I went into seclusion and chose to grieve alone and over some time it became extremely unhealthy. Grieving was all I could do— I was in mourning. As I lay in bed one evening a boisterous voice screamed out to me. It told me, "Get up and get going!" It was a like a jolt of lightning that came from the unknown and shook me awake; I got dressed and headed for the front door. My first instinct led me to the local bookstore (that was odd because I rarely go there). Bernadette had been raving about a book called *Heaven is for Real*. She told me to read it because she felt the book could possibly help me through my pain. After finding the title I started to make my way to the checkout counter. However, my caffeine addiction kicked in and luckily I noticed the café nearby. After grabbing my coffee fix, I decided to read for a while. I was heading for a table when I noticed an interesting looking man sitting nearby (I also noticed that he had the type of computer I was interested in buying). I sat down at the table next to him in hopes of learning about the computer. He looked up and smiled.

I said, "Hi".

He politely answered, "Hey, how are you?"

I asked, "How do you like that computer? I've been researching that model for a while but I'm not sure what type to get."

"I like it. I use it for most things. It fits me pretty well," he answered.

We began an easy conversation. He started by telling me what he did for a living and why he chose that computer. I found it surprisingly easy to strike up a conversation with him.

He asked, "What are you reading there?"

"It's called, *Heaven is for Real*. My mother recently passed and my sister felt that I should read it in hopes that I could benefit from the message."

The stranger's way intrigued me. There was a hint of shyness within him and I felt he wouldn't have talked to me if I didn't initiate things. After we spoke for a while the store was about to close so I gathered my things to leave. He asked me what I did for a living and then asked if I might be interested in playing a little golf sometime. Although paradise is considered the Mecca of golf, I let him know I usually couldn't find time to swing my clubs.

I said, "Yeah. I golf from time to time, but not too often".

With kind eyes he said, "Well maybe we can get together and loose some golf balls."

I'm always up for making new friends so we exchanged numbers and planned on setting a date to play. About a week passed when my phone rang, however, I missed the call. After checking my voicemail I learned that the nice shy man, Justin, had tried to call. He was interested in some golf so I let him know I was up for the challenge. Before we went to an actual course, Justin thought it might be best to go to a driving range first (I still believe he just wanted to test my golfing skills). I'm not the avid golfer but I feel I impressed my new friend. After swinging the clubs for a while we decided to grab a quick liquid lunch.

Our conversations were always entertaining. We talked at ease about a variety of things: our pasts, our goals for the future and Justin made it point to keep things a little silly. The next week we headed out to a major course, all the while cracking jokes and making fun of each other's golf swing (Justin thought it was pretty easy to tease me). At one particular hole we were waiting patiently to tee off when the needling continued.

"So smarty pants, what was your major in school?" I asked.

He answered, "Journalism and some graphic design. I'm no Burroughs but I enjoy writing from time to time."

"No shit!" I blurted out.

He told me about a few of his writing aspirations and that being involved in writing a book was certainly one of them.

I shot back, "That's great! I've always wanted to write a book as well. I've been encouraged to write my life's story. Well, why don't we get started?"

I figured he'd dismiss the idea because we had just met, but I was delightfully mistaken.

He didn't bat an eyelash and said, "That would be great Mary. I'd love to help you out."

As new writing partners we started to hash out some ideas and the wheels were in motion. After that round of golf I headed home to collect my thoughts and think about prospective story ideas. As I sat on my bed I couldn't think of a better source to ask advice from, then God himself. I needed a little divine intervention to get myself going in order to write this book, so I quickly sparked up a Godly banter. My quasi-metaphysical dialogue went something like this:

I asked, "God, I believe you brought Justin into my life to help me write this book. I've wanted to write for quite some time and I feel that I'm ready. What do you think?"

He immediately answered, "Yes. It's about time. But you must realize that your writing will not only be for you but it is mainly for me."

I was astounded and asked, "What on earth do you mean?"

"I need you to help me as a messenger in writing this book. I also believe you will gain a spiritual connection throughout the creative process. This will be an incredible lesson for you Mary," God said.

It took me a few moments to process what I thought God was saying to me. When I finally decided to write this book in no way did I expect or want to act as a messenger for God. The spiritual implications were confusing – I first thought that my stories would be focused on my career experiences (and to hopefully aid young people as a mentor). Also, a goal of mine has been for this project to serve as a vehicle to share future motivational stories; this new direction and spiritual implications have stirred my creative juices. I have always been confident in my relationship with God but I just wasn't quite sure how I could help others connect with our Creator in a similar way. Finally, after thinking about the situation I said to my-self, "Alright... you're on. Let's do it."

Writing about some of my experiences has become one of those 'experiences of a lifetime' for Justin and me. I've learned that he has a wonderful ability of taking my stories and adding dimension to them, all the while maintaining their integrity.   At times this experience makes me feel like I'm learning a mystical dance for the first time; however, it's a dance that we've trained for forever. We laugh often and have bonded closely through this journey. At times we act as each other's guide and it truly feels like we'll be in each other's lives forever, no matter what the design may be. Although he is shy at times, I feel Justin will be able to handle any attention this project might bring about. God will help him along the path.

Justin J is my champion and my angel. In return – I am his. It is safe to say I couldn't have written this without his help – and for that I am extremely grateful.

(Side note: I find it funny that his initials are JC and my name is Mary. God send?).

INNER MISSIONS

The following missions are personal goals from ACTS IV that I aim to embrace.

Acceptance: To faithfully walk our unique life path and fearlessly embrace the passage to our next life through death.

 Choices: Love through the hurt and forgive through the pain.

Truth: The gifts of life are attained through our level of fearlessness.

Sharing: Want for nothing and believe in attaining everything through faith.

I Believe

Waking up in the middle of the night has become a common occurrence for me. One of those random nights I had a dream and received a message that will always play vividly in my mind. Upon awaking with a jolt, beads of sweat formed on my face and I began to breathe heavily as I was consumed with panic. I sat upright and my mind was instantly overwrought with fear. It was apparent that the dream's message was so powerfully intense that my subconscious blasted me awake.

I asked myself, "What am I doing?"

I was upset and physically shaking. Earlier that evening Justin and I had an editing session on the book and it dawned on me just how much I was beginning to question this project. Extremely quiet and sullenly sitting across from him, my writing partner noticed the difference. Kindly, he asked if there was any trouble. I blew it off and said no, but my conscience was telling me differently. It was quite obvious that second-guessing this project was settling in and was beginning to show.

In that impressionable dream that had awoken me, I asked God, "What if people judge me and don't like what I have to say? Worse yet, what if they don't get the message I'm helping you to spread?"

After waking up I couldn't stop hyperventilating and the blood began to race through my veins. Then in an instant, my breathing slowed considerably as my heart started to beat smoothly. Finally – I could think clearly. I got up, went into the bathroom and looked in the mirror.

I asked myself, "Was I asking God for guidance in my dream? Why should I be the one to write this book for God and my parents?"

As soon as I asked the question my conversation with God started.

Straight and right to the point – he told me, "Your answer is in the first paragraph of your book."

God said, "I knew you would choose to take action and write."

"Don't you think there are millions of people who have wanted to write a book but never did? People out there who have been told they should write a book but never followed through with it? Those people never wrote because they didn't believe they had an important message – or they didn't believe they had what it took. I knew you would have the courage and faith to make the choice to write. It is your belief in your life's design that powers your dedication. Mary, you were born believing not only in me, but in how powerful a person's choices are in designing their lives," God explained.

"Wow. I'm starting to understand much better now," I said.

God continued to say, "You see – my message can be understood by answering this question: if you believe in a creator, then why wouldn't I create a universe that would grant all that you need? The only way to tap into that supply of endless gifts is to truly believe. Then, you must choose to move forward and work towards whatever it is that you may want in life. I came to you because you would do just that: believe in a divine power that is manifested through hard work and faith."

I asked God, "That's a lot of trust for you to have in me, isn't it?"

God then asked, "Haven't you always strived to make honest choices in your life? For instance: taking back the apple after you wrongfully took it. That was an honest choice. Also, you decided against ending your pregnancy and give birth to Blake and have faith that it would end with an incredible gift. Wasn't it you who chose to leave a high level position because it didn't reflect who you were? And didn't you decide to go to Minnesota for medical care, even though you were extremely tired and fearful?"

He continued, "One of the most important choices you've made was to believe in your mother's decision to move to the next life. Also, you knew it to be true that I wouldn't let her suffer through her transition. Furthermore, you chose to believe in all things that allowed you to receive some of life's greatest gifts even if the path was fraught with hurt and pain."

I said, "Yes, I most certainly was. Can I ask you a question? Is one of your messages for people to believe in their choices and then to reap the benefits?"

God answered, "Yes, it's that simple. One of the most mysterious gifts someone can be given is the strength to believe enough to step outside of themselves and allow the universe to open up to them. Human beings often make life difficult by filling it with doubt and fear. At one time or another almost everyone deals with challenging situations in a negative way and those negative choices can make us suffer. Not only do you suffer, but the people around you begin to suffer as well. You all feel that in some way you were meant to struggle and it is that very ideology that couldn't be further from the truth. Mary, can you think of a time when you haven't really attained what you wanted?"

"Well, not really," I said.

God continued, "The journey may have been different than you thought, but the end results were always what you really wanted. A person's choices drive them through life on earth. Why not approach living life with a voracity that is fueled by faith? Why not live with passion? Why would you want to be born and live on this wonderful planet any other way?"

I said sarcastically, "Well, this is some monumental thinking even in its most simplistic terms… isn't it?"

"No, you make it that way," God explained. "Isn't what I'm describing here the way in which your mother lived her entire life? Living life with passionate faith was second nature to her; that is how she approached living every day. It may not be easy to understand but all people have to do is step outside of themselves, believe, practice patience and trust that we will make it happen together. The journey might not be exactly what you thought; but you will glean the inevitable. I promise."

"So – life is all about choices?" I asked.

"Yes," God told me. "Make the choice to move forward with this book and you will see. You will see that together we will get our message into the hands of the people who will benefit from it. The plan is already in place."

God then said with strong guidance, "So please live through your choices and believe that your plan is in motion. Remember – your father and you always said: 'I believe'."

I went back to bed, woke up the next morning and told Justin that there was one last chapter that needed to be written. I chose to title it: "I Believe!"

End scene.

Epilogue

I would like to thank many people for their love and support. My family is first on the list of the many whom I need to graciously thank for showering me with love and guidance. To my brothers, sisters and their spouses—thank you. I love you all dearly.

I also want to thank my sons for loving me even when I faltered. God truly blessed me when he gave me my boys. Thank you to my nieces and nephews who are actually like brothers and sisters to me. I also want to thank my friends whom I consider my extended family; they are next to none and I can always count on their incredible support.

To my friend Father Ed: you are such a caring and loving priest who spreads the all-powerful message of God through true faith. Thank you for being there for our mother in her transition from this earth. I know you have to put up with a lot of challenging conversations with your friend Mary, but please know those conversations are born out of my complete respect for you.

I would like to thank Patrick not only for being one of my best friends but also for serving our country without question. You are truly a selfless being. To Justin, I can't wait to see what gifts God has in store for you – I believe so much fun awaits us.

Most of all I want to say thank you to my parents. St. Bernice and Henry have and always will be my blissful rays of sunshine that will continue to guide my life's design. They are parents, mentors and my best friends. I love them deeply and make sure to talk with them every day. God only knows how great my love is for my parents. There will never be a passing moment that I don't think of them. As the sun rises and sets, I will always be talking to you with the help of our Creator.

After living this experience and completing this new adventure, I have found a new passion: a passion for writing. My plans are not to stop with this book but to write others. Writing (no matter how good or bad) always grants me with an incredible sense of fun. As I write all I think to do is – 'just live it'.

These pages contain my life laid down through writing. I hope you've enjoyed not only reading this book, but observed many helpful lessons unfold. A memoir is about one's life and now after writing this, I have finally realized why I've lived my life the way I have. I've tried to live the way my mother has taught me: to live and share the gifts we have all received. My mother taught my family how God means for us to live. It is through her message, or you could say her Inner-Missions, that she showed us the way by faithfully living her life and fearlessly living her death. In a sense, her life's road map showed so many people their own way. Mom illustrated that people are meant to mold and create their destiny and that life will continue on through death. In knowing that, I recognize that there are changes I need to make in my life to accomplish my spiritual aspirations.

I have faith that there may be an enlightenment that will take place and knowing that, it is clear that everyday ACTS affect not only the individual but also the people we love (and perhaps those we don't even know).

I hope that by sharing my experiences, my mom's life and her passing, that it will lead the way for more people to recognize the blessings that come with a relationship with our creator. God wants us to know that there are millions of ways to live and die with love, truth and joy. He grants us a myriad number of avenues to attain happiness and perhaps most importantly, to live with respect and make choices that truly represent who we are.

I know that it is far easier for people to look back and only recount their positive choices. I tell you here, that it is far more challenging to be up front and honest about things we'd like to be different. When I think of what I'd like to change in my life, I'd like my commitments to my creator, myself and all of you to be strengthened. You will learn what my commitments are when you read my Final ACTS.

It is an honor to know that you have picked up this book and read it from cover to cover. I hope that you have genuinely gained something from this experience.

To my mother I say, "Raise both hands and I will raise mine as we high ten together and say, '**We are all in**'."

I now exit stage right by asking all of you these final questions. What are your Inner-Missions? What are your ACTS? Moving forward, how do you plan to attain your life's missions? As you do so, I would love to hear about your accomplishments and how you create your own paradise. If you would like, please share them with me on the Designing Your Life Facebook page @ www.facebook.com/DesigningYourLifeBook

I know that God is honored and loves you all very much for making the choices you've made. He too looks forward to sharing your experiences while you are '**Designing Your Life**'.

FINAL ACTS

ACCEPTANCE: THAT WE ARE
          ALL CONNECTED

CHOICES: TO DESIGN MY LIFE

TRUTH: TO LIVE FAITHFULLY

SHARING: TO LOOK INWARD
          FOR CHANGE.

TO BE JOYFUL

www.ingramcontent.com/pod-product-compliance
Lightning Source LLC
Chambersburg PA
CBHW030936150426
42812CB00064B/2942/J